WHAT PEOPLE ARE SAYING ABOUT KYNAN BRIDGES AND HIS BOOKS...

INVADING THE HEAVENS

Anyone looking for a genuine supernatural breakthrough—in any area of their lives—should read *Invading the Heavens* by Kynan Bridges. His first chapter is called "Anatomy of a Breakthrough," and the whole book unfolds the various features of the divine plan for accessing heavenly freedom and blessings. With wisdom, humor, and clear illustrations, Kynan explains what a breakthrough is and how to position yourself to receive one, as you live from God's presence 24/7. The open heavens are available to all believers—but an open heaven demands an open earth. This book shows how to break through the barriers and hindrances in your life to receive all that your heavenly Father has promised you. As you read *Invading the Heavens*, allow the revelation to become your manifestation!

—Joshua Mills
Author, *Power Portals* and *Moving in Glory Realms*
International Glory Ministries, Palm Springs, CA
www.JoshuaMills.com

For all of us, it is part of the human condition to face limitation. One of the most important ways in which certain limitations are transcended is by the effect our prayers have. God has ordained prayer as a way for things to be transformed. Fervent prayer, rooted in faith, gets a response from the triune God and brings about what Kynan Bridges refers to as "breakthrough." This new book, *Invading the Heavens*, is from a series of sermons that Kynan preached. It invites you into that most sacred conversation the Scriptures refer to as prayer, so that in that conversation you might transcend those limitations that are impeding your walk with the God who called you into the conversation to transform you into His image and likeness.

—Bishop Mark J. Chironna
Church On the Living Edge
Mark Ch᠎᠎᠎᠎᠎᠎᠎᠎᠎᠎᠎᠎᠎FL

Kynan Bridges has written a great book full of insight on achieving the breakthroughs we as the body of Christ desperately need today. *Invading the Heavens* contains a treasure trove of golden nuggets of wisdom that together provide a spiritual framework for entering into maturity and experiencing all God intended us to have. I suggest that every believer who yearns for more than they are now experiencing should read this book. It contains the direction you are looking for and will change your life.

—*Joan Hunter*
Author/Healing Evangelist
Joanhunter.org

KINGDOM AUTHORITY

Prophetic voices are rising up, pronouncing a third Great Awakening, but pushing back the darkness demands a revelation of our authority in Christ. In his book *Kingdom Authority*, Kynan Bridges offers a fresh perspective on an ancient truth about the believer's position of power in a raging spiritual war. He equips you to stand up and fight for the promises of God for your life, your city, and your nation.

—*Jennifer LeClaire*
News Editor, *Charisma* magazine
Author, *The Spiritual Warrior's Guide to Defeating Jezebel*
Director, Awakening House of Prayer, Ft. Lauderdale, FL

Kynan Bridges stirs up a passion and hunger within the heart of the believer to long for and see the glory of God! He prepares the body of Christ to get ready to see our all-powerful God work in our lives and manifest His glory and kingdom.

—*Dr. Jeremy Lopez*
CEO, IdentityNetwork.net

Pastor Kynan Bridges has done it again! The revelation of the Word that he shares will give you keys to mighty kingdom realities. As you apply the revelations he teaches, you will find the power of God to literally erase the borders of the impossible. And as you follow the truths that Pastor Bridges presents, you will deepen your relationship with the Father and the Son and, in the process, discover your authority to disarm, defeat, and demolish the powers of darkness! You have been given authority over the spirits of darkness so that souls might be saved, sick bodies might be healed, and people's lives might be transformed for the glory of God.

—*Pastor Tony Kemp*
President, ACTS Group
Vice President, *It's Supernatural!* and ISN Network

THE POWER OF PROPHETIC PRAYER

Want to be more effective in prayer? Want to make history before the throne of God? Want to learn from a veteran champion and not a novice? Then go no further! Destiny is staring you right in the face through the life, ministry, and writings of Kynan Bridges. *The Power of Prophetic Prayer* will definitely increase the level of revelation in your life, give you strategic understanding of the practical how-to's of prayer, and propel you into prayers that strike the mark!

—*Dr. James W. Goll*
Founder, God Encounters Ministries
International best-selling author

Kynan Bridges is one of my favorite Bible teachers. We are on the precipice of the greatest revival and move of miracles in history. This book will "make sure" you fulfill your prophetic destiny.

—*Sid Roth*
Host, *It's Supernatural!*

UNMASKING THE ACCUSER

Why be duped by the devil? Dr. Kynan Bridges' book does a powerful job of unmasking the Accuser—Satan. You will be amazed by what the devil's been up to in your life and in your church! This book is an incredible tool for fighting the 'nice' sins inside the church that cause such division: slander, gossip, and offense. With kingdom authority and pastoral power, *Unmasking the Accuser* shows the danger of lending an ear to evil and shows the blessing of choosing Christ instead. The revelation in this book will expose Satan, challenge believers—and change your life!

—*Bishop George G. Bloomer*
Best-selling author, *Witchcraft in the Pews*
Pastor, Bethel Family Worship Center, Durham, NC

Kynan Bridges has a wonderful ability to articulate biblical truth. He gets straight to the point, deals with the thorniest of issues, and applies God's remedy. *Unmasking the Accuser* is no exception as it exposes the root of so many issues and snares that rob us of victory. Read this practical book, receive the truth, and get ready to walk in a new level of freedom and power!

—*Aliss Cresswell*
Director, Spirit Lifestyle and Morning Star Europe

UNLOCKING THE CODE OF THE SUPERNATURAL

THE SECRET TO GOD'S POWER IN YOU

KYNAN BRIDGES

WHITAKER HOUSE

Unless otherwise indicated, all Scripture quotations are taken from the *King James Version Easy Read Bible*, KJVER®, © 2001, 2007, 2010, 2015 by Whitaker House. Used by permission. All rights reserved. Scripture quotations marked (NKJV) are taken from the *New King James Version*, © 1979, 1980, 1982 by Thomas Nelson, Inc. Used by permission. All rights reserved.

Boldface type in the Scripture quotations indicates the author's emphasis. The forms LORD and GOD (in small capital letters) in Bible quotations represent the Hebrew name for God *Yahweh* (Jehovah), while *Lord* and *God* normally represent the name *Adonai*, in accordance with the Bible version used.

Some definitions of Greek words are taken from the New Testament Greek Lexicon—King James Version or New American Standard, based on Thayer's and Smith's Bible Dictionary, plus others (public domain), www.BibleStudyTools.com. Some definitions of Hebrew words are taken from the Old Testament Hebrew Lexicon—King James Version or New American Standard, which is the Brown, Driver, Briggs, Gesenius Lexicon (public domain), BibleStudyTools.com. Other Greek and Hebrew definitions are taken from the electronic version of *Strong's Exhaustive Concordance of the Bible*, STRONG, (© 1980, 1986, and assigned to World Bible Publishers, Inc. Used by permission. All rights reserved.).

Unless otherwise indicated, all dictionary definitions are taken from Lexico.com, Oxford University Press, © 2020.

UNLOCKING THE CODE OF THE SUPERNATURAL:
The Secret to God's Power in You

Kynan Bridges Ministries, Inc.
P.O. Box 159
Ruskin, FL 33575
www.kynanbridges.com
info@kynanbridges.com

ISBN: 978-1-64123-580-8 • eBook ISBN: 978-1-64123-581-5
Printed in the United States of America
© 2021 by Kynan Bridges

Whitaker House
1030 Hunt Valley Circle • New Kensington, PA 15068
www.whitakerhouse.com

Library of Congress Control Number: 2020948833

1 2 3 4 5 6 7 8 9 10 11 12 ⨄ 29 28 27 26 25 24 23 22 21

CONTENTS

PREFACE: THE NEW-CREATION LIFE

God wants us to live a supernatural lifestyle, full of His grace and power! He wants us to be free of problems that hinder us from moving forward in life, such as fear, guilt, and depression. He desires that we move in miracles, signs, and wonders as we expand His kingdom on earth.

However, many believers never enter into a supernatural lifestyle because they are held back by false ideas of what it means to be a Christian, how they should relate to their heavenly Father, and how to be led by the Spirit—misconceptions that have been entrenched in their minds for years.

What will unlock the code of the supernatural in our lives, enabling us to live a dynamic, Spirit-filled life?

Through my study of God's Word, personal experiences, and ministry to thousands of Christians, I have found that when we don't have a clear understanding of what it means to be brand-new in Christ, we block the flow of God's Spirit within us. Unless we truly know who we are in Jesus, we will lack confidence in His ability to work miracles through us. If we rely on our own efforts rather than the power of the Holy Spirit within us, we will constantly be frustrated. If we feel trapped and condemned by our past, believing God will never be able to use us because of our bad choices or failures—or what others have done to us—we will be hindered from walking in the supernatural.

I have designed this book to unveil the various facets of what it means to be a new creation in Christ and live according to the Spirit. We will look at a number of key Scriptures, especially from the Gospels and the Epistles, that relate to this theme. These Scriptures, reviewed in sequence, will strengthen our understanding of our life in Christ, reinforcing vital biblical truths until we gain a full picture of our spiritual newness. In this way, with each chapter, we will progressively renew our minds to unlock the code of the supernatural and find the secret to God's power in us.

As we enter the supernatural lifestyle God desires for us, one of the most difficult hurdles we will need to overcome is a religious spirit, which can easily sneak into our lives in a number of ways. However, by the power of God's Spirit and the transformation of our minds, we can break free of this stronghold. We will look at this essential topic throughout several chapters in part I of this book.

I learned the spiritual lessons that I share in these pages over the course of many years. It was not an overnight process but rather a journey involving questions, doubts, struggles, and reorientation from incorrect mindsets to the truth of God's Word. This journey opened up an amazing, miraculous lifestyle for me—one that is available to *all* believers. While we each need to go through a process of renewing our minds, I pray that the truths I present will shorten the length of your own journey so you can quickly move into a daily living relationship with your heavenly Father, moving from flesh to Spirit, from doubt to faith, from defeat to victory, and from natural to supernatural.

Unlocking the Code of the Supernatural covers such matters as our identity in Christ, who Jesus really is, Christ-consciousness versus sin-consciousness, the consequences of the religious spirit, breaking the cycle of striving, recreation verses reformation, the Spirit-filled life, accepting our position of righteousness, living from the inside-out, and much more. I have included testimonies from my life and others' lives that demonstrate God's supernatural power to bring healing and transformation. Additionally, at the ends of the chapters, I have provided

"Victory Prayers" and "Insights" questions so you can immediately apply what you are learning to your life.

You may never have moved in a miraculous lifestyle. Or, perhaps you have experienced moments of supernatural power and victory but haven't been able to reach the next level in your spiritual walk or expand your faith for greater works in God's Spirit. This book will enable you to recognize and overcome areas that have been holding you back. It will show you the secret to God's power in you and the manifestation of God's kingdom in the world. *Unlocking the Code of the Supernatural* will free you to live as the ever-new, unique creation God designed and redeemed you to be!

PART I:
BIRTHED INTO THE SUPERNATURAL!

FIRST THINGS FIRST

*"But we speak the wisdom of God in a mystery, even the hidden
wisdom, which God ordained before the world to our glory."*
—1 Corinthians 2:7

I was sitting with my mother in the living room of our home in Georgia.
We were watching Christian television, as was her custom. That particular
afternoon, a popular televangelist was talking about heaven and salvation.
I vividly remember the speaker giving an invitation for people to be saved. I
asked my mother, "Can I be saved? Can I go to heaven?" She replied, "Yes,"
and I said the prayer of salvation. I was nine years old.

A RADICAL TRANSFORMATION

This was my first encounter with Jesus. I was excited about the idea
that when I died, I would go to a very special place called heaven, and I
would be with the Lord for all eternity. It was comforting to know that I
wouldn't have to spend an eternity in a devil's hell! Little did I know what
I had gotten myself into when I prayed that prayer. I had no idea what the
full ramifications of being a believer were. No one really told me about

discipleship, faith, baptism, or Spirit-filled living. I was just glad to be going to heaven.

Following my salvation, I grew and matured in my faith through a profound, life-changing process that spanned a number of years, with various stops and starts along the way. Through this process, I came to discover that becoming a Christian was about much more than saying a prayer so you can go to heaven. In the new birth, God has literally given us an entirely *brand-new, supernatural nature*, and this nature has the power to impact every area of our lives. Being a believer is not a religious experience—it is a mystery involving a radical transformation of our spiritual DNA. In *Unlocking the Code of the Supernatural*, we will explore this radical transformation and its implications for supernatural living.

> BEING A CHRISTIAN IS NOT A RELIGIOUS EXPERIENCE—
> IT IS A MYSTERY INVOLVING A RADICAL TRANSFORMATION
> OF OUR SPIRITUAL DNA.

"THE WISDOM OF GOD IN A MYSTERY"

What is this spiritual "mystery" of the new-creation life? One dictionary definition of *mystery* is "something that is difficult or impossible to understand or explain." Does this mean I am saying the Christian life is hard to comprehend? No, that is not the type of mystery I am referring to. The biblical meaning of *"mystery"* is totally different from our common understanding of this word. In 1 Corinthians, the apostle Paul gives us insight into the mystery of the Christian life:

But we speak the wisdom of God in a mystery, even the hidden wisdom, which God ordained before the world to our glory.
—1 Corinthians 2:7

In the original Greek, Paul uses the word *mysterion*, which can refer to "the secret counsels which govern God in dealing with the righteous, which are hidden from ungodly and wicked men but plain to the godly." In other words, the mystery of a Christian's new nature can only be revealed to those who believe. The world cannot comprehend what it means to be born again. It is not something people can fathom unless they receive illumination by the Holy Spirit, who is God's gift to us at salvation.

Jesus said the Holy Spirit would guide us into all truth. (See John 16:13.) As believers, we need to understand what it really means to have a new life in Christ because it is our spiritual inheritance to comprehend this new life and act on it. When we receive this understanding, it will totally change the way we see ourselves and the way we live.

LIVING VICTORIOUSLY

As I described above, even though a mysterious transformation had occurred within me when, as a boy, I received a new life in Jesus Christ, I didn't have a clue what had really transpired. I was just happy to be going to heaven. My joy in my salvation was certainly real and appropriate. However, I did not yet grasp all that God had given me. This was natural because I was only a child and also brand-new in my faith. Yet it would not have been natural for me to have remained in that limited understanding. Spiritual growth was necessary for me to enter into the supernatural life God had given me and wanted me to walk in.

Unfortunately, many believers today haven't progressed further in their understanding of the profound transformation that has occurred within them than their initial salvation. And they are not children, but rather pastors, evangelists, elders, choir directors, ushers, deacons, and churchgoers who have never fully tapped into what God has given them. They haven't discovered the nature of this spiritual mystery, even decades after receiving Christ. This message isn't being taught or practiced in a widespread way in the church. As a result, these believers are missing out on a dynamic lifestyle filled with blessing and victory.

The church often tries to convince the world that we serve a God who is alive, and yet when people visit a church service on a Sunday morning, they often see a gathering of people in which the life and power of God seem to be absent. What is missing? Why are so many Christians living lives of defeat and bondage? Why are there people in the church who struggle with ongoing sin in their lives? Where is the authority and power to live the victorious life we read about in the Bible? Is there more to the Christian life than being involved in nice programs and events in our local church community? The answer is found in what it means to be a new creation in Christ. There is a correlation between understanding the mystery of the new nature and living victoriously. The purpose of this book is to encourage you to live a life that transcends what you can see and feel so you can tap into a supernatural reality that is so tremendous, it will knock you out of your seat!

If the majority of Christians fully understood what it means to have a brand-new, supernatural nature, it would change the landscape of the church forever because this is the secret to God's power within us. We would know how God really feels about us, why He sent His Son to die on the cross, and the implications of our being filled with His Spirit. Imagine a church that is overflowing with whole, Spirit-filled, life-giving believers who walk in power and authority! A church where people are completely confident and conscious of their identity in Christ. Where they have a thorough knowledge of who Jesus is and who they are in Him—and they spread this exciting message to the world!

WHAT IS YOUR EXPERIENCE OF THE CHRISTIAN LIFE? ARE YOU WALKING IN CONFIDENCE AND POWER, WITH THE KNOWLEDGE OF WHO YOU ARE IN CHRIST?

WHO IS JESUS, REALLY?

Paul again wrote about the *"mystery"* of the new-creation life in his letter to the Colossians:

Whereof [the church] I am made a minister, according to the dispensation of God which is given to me for you, to fulfill the word of God; even the mystery which has been hidden from ages and from generations, but now is made manifest to His saints: to whom God would make known what is the riches of the glory of this mystery among the Gentiles; which is Christ in you, the hope of glory.
—Colossians 1:25–27

When we become new creations, Christ comes to live within us in all His fullness. In the above passage, the word translated *"mystery"* is the same Greek word we looked at earlier: *mysterion.* We need the Holy Spirit to illuminate us regarding what it means for Christ, *"the hope of glory,"* to dwell within us.

To comprehend this *"mystery,"* we must first recognize who Jesus really is—who it is that dwells within us. A knowledge of Jesus may seem basic and self-explanatory. However, you may be surprised at the number of people who actually lack this knowledge, even though they profess to be Christians. Religion and tradition have done much to shape people's false conceptions of Jesus. Many individuals think of Jesus Christ as a religious relic. Others essentially think of Him as a more sophisticated version of Santa Claus. But the Bible tells us exactly who Jesus is:

In the beginning was the Word, and the Word was with God, and the Word was God. The same was in the beginning with God. All things were made by Him; and without Him was not any thing made that was made. In Him was life; and the life was the light of men. And the light shines in darkness; and the darkness comprehended it not.
—John 1:1–5

In this familiar passage of Scripture, the apostle John uses some significant terminology in reference to Jesus. First, he tells us that Jesus *"was in the beginning"* and *"was God."* Therefore, we know that Jesus was preexistent and coequal with the Father. In addition to emphasizing that Christ existed with God in the beginning, John uses this intriguing title to describe Him: *"the Word."*

"Word" is translated from the Greek word *logos*, which is a difficult concept to explain in contemporary English. In the sense of speech, *logos* refers to "a word, uttered by a living voice, [that] embodies a conception or idea." John's use of the word *logos* reveals that God created the invisible and visible universe through the person of the living Word, Jesus Christ. This fact is noteworthy because words give form and purpose to the world around us. Words are used to describe reality. When we want to describe a person or thing, we must express the nature of that entity through language. In His sovereignty, God chose to create everything that exists through the Word. From the beginning, He saw creation in the context of His Son.

Jesus is not merely a religious symbol or a good Teacher. He actually gives form, purpose, and substance to everything in creation! This is the same Jesus whom we worship at church every Sunday. Thus, in John 1, the Holy Spirit makes a point to help us understand Jesus's true nature and identity. Again, if we are to have a genuine relationship with Jesus Christ, we must know who He is.

JESUS GIVES FORM, PURPOSE, AND SUBSTANCE TO EVERYTHING IN CREATION!

If John had stopped there in his description of Jesus, it might have sufficed, but he did not. He went on to tell us that *"all things were made by [Christ]; and without Him was not any thing made that was made."* Not only was Jesus the means of creation, but nothing at all would exist in the created world without Him. He literally created everything. The Greek word translated *"made"* in this passage is *ginomai*. This is the term from which the word *gene* and *genome* are derived. A genome is defined as "the complete set of genes or genetic material present in a cell or organism." You could say that Christ is the "basic material" by which all things are created and sustained. Paul puts it this way in Colossians 1:17:

He is before all things, and by Him all things consist.

The Greek word rendered *"consist"* is *synistemi,* among whose meanings is "to bring or band together." When we combine the ideas of these two Greek words, *ginomai* and *synistemi,* we see that Christ is the source from which everything has its genesis, and He is also the bonding agent by which the very fiber of the universe is held together.

The word rendered *"made"* in John 1 is a transliteration of the Hebrew term for *"made"* found in Genesis 1 in reference to God as Creator. From these few verses of Scripture, we can deduce that Christ is our Creator, Definer, Purpose, and Sustainer. When we consider the implications of this reality, it is mind-blowing.

WHEN IS THE LAST TIME YOU THOUGHT OF

JESUS AS THE ONE WHO HOLDS THE VERY FIBER

OF YOUR BEING TOGETHER?

This would be enough information about Jesus to ponder for a millennium, but the apostle John continues, revealing even more about Him. John 1:4 says, *"In Him was life; and the life was the light of men."* What exactly does this mean? The term translated *"life"* here is *zoe*, which refers to "the absolute fullness of life, both essential and ethical, which belongs to God, and through him both to the hypostatic 'logos' and to Christ in whom the 'logos' put on human nature."

This divine fullness is the nature of the *"life"* that is *"the light of men."* Verse 9 tells us, *"That was the true Light, which lights every man that comes into the world."* Jesus, the Light, illuminates spiritual truth to us, and He affects every person who has ever come into the world. The atheist and the agnostic are without excuse before God because the very fact that they exist testifies to the Creator.

Thus, Christ is Creator, Definer, Purpose, Sustainer, Life, and Light for humanity. Does this mean I received the fullness of God's life when I prayed to receive Christ in my living room as a boy? Absolutely! And, if you have sincerely accepted Jesus Christ as your Lord and Savior, you have received these spiritual riches as well. Through Christ, we have access to the fullness of divine life.

> CHRIST IS OUR CREATOR, DEFINER, PURPOSE, AND SUSTAINER. WHEN WE TRULY CONSIDER THE IMPLICATIONS OF THIS REALITY, IT IS MIND-BLOWING.

DANGEROUSLY NEW CREATIONS!

These truths about who Christ is and what it means that He dwells within us by His Holy Spirit have profound implications for living a supernatural lifestyle. Have you ever wondered why the church at large does not walk in the level of supernatural power that the early church did? It is principally because they don't recognize the power that is resident within them! Have you ever questioned why there has been a surge of interest in mysticism and the occult in the Western world? The truth is that people are searching for the supernatural. As created beings, we seem to be wired for it.

Unfortunately, whole denominations in the Christian church have come up with convenient theological frameworks that are, at best, dismissive of the reality of the supernatural. Some people assert that the gifts of the Spirit went out of operation after the age of the early apostles or that there is no longer any need for the miraculous because the Bible gives us everything we require for our spiritual lives. If you have subscribed to one of these viewpoints, let me encourage you to look again at what the Scriptures say. Don't allow yourself to be in denial regarding the ways God desires to move in, and work through, His people.

The reality is that Jesus Christ shed His precious blood for our sins and was raised from the dead so that we could walk in supernatural newness of life in the power of the Holy Spirit. When we understand this truth, we have the potential to be overcomers who live in victory and are detrimental to Satan's kingdom of darkness. We will be "ticking time bombs" that destroy the enemy's schemes wherever we go. We will be filled with wisdom and knowledge concerning our Creator and all He made us to be. Simply put, we will be dangerously new creations!

VICTORY PRAYER

Father, in the name of Jesus Christ, I thank You for who You are and all You have done for me. I believe that Jesus is the Son of God and that, through His blood, I am a new creation. Thank You that my entire purpose for living comes from You. I know that, through Jesus, You created everything that exists, including me. Jesus is my Creator, Definer, Purpose, Sustainer, Life, and Light. Thank You, Lord, for unfolding the mystery of Your wisdom as I release my faith in You and follow Your plans for me. I declare that the mystery of Jesus is unveiled in my spirit. In Jesus's name, amen!

If you have never before received Christ, I invite you to pray this prayer and enter into a new life in Him!

Heavenly Father, I recognize that I am a sinner in desperate need of a Savior. I believe that Jesus Christ is Your Son. I believe that He suffered on the cross and died for me, descended into hell and defeated Satan, and now sits at Your right hand praying for me so that I may have abundant life. I am sorry for my sins; I repent of them and renounce them. Through the blood of Christ, I ask You to forgive me of all of my sins—those that are known to me and those that are unknown to me.

I receive Jesus as my Lord and Savior, and I give Him complete control over my life. I want to live for You from my innermost being and in every area of my life. I renounce Satan and all of his wicked works. I divorce myself from his evil influence. Lord, I recognize that I cannot live for You in my own strength. I ask You to fill me with Your precious Holy Spirit and give me the gift of speaking in other tongues, as the Spirit gives utterance, as the initial evidence of a transformed life. I ask this in the name of Your Son, Jesus Christ, amen!

UNLOCKING THE CODE OF THE SUPERNATURAL INSIGHTS

1. What is the reason many believers haven't made much progress in understanding the nature of their new birth since their salvation? In what ways might you need to grow in your comprehension of what transpired when you received Jesus?

2. How does the biblical definition of "mystery" compare to the common definition of this term?

3. List some titles that describe the nature of Jesus Christ, based on the first chapter of John. How do these titles help you to understand who Jesus really is?

4. Name some characteristics of the church when it is functioning in the way it is meant to.

MIRACLE TESTIMONY

RECEIVING A BRAND-NEW MIND

While I was growing up, I struggled tremendously in school. I was told by the board of education that I had attention deficit hyperactivity disorder (ADHD). I had a very difficult time paying attention and remembering what was taught in class. This led to many problems: I daydreamed all the time. I fought with other students. I was profane.

However, when I gave my life to Christ, something supernatural happened within me. I literally received a new mind. God's DNA was deposited into my very being. After this, I began to think and reason differently. My paradigm changed, and thus my worldview was transformed. I continually reminded myself that I had the mind of Christ. Although some people had told me that I would never graduate from high school, I was supernaturally able to graduate, and I was also accepted at a university. Today, I have several academic degrees, and I have written a number of books. Glory to God for the power of the new creation!

2

A NEW CREATION

"If any man be in Christ, he is a new creature ["creation," NKJV]: old things are passed away; behold, all things are become new."
—2 Corinthians 5:17

What does the Bible mean when it speaks of our being a *"new creation"*? The answer to this question has both philosophical and practical significance. Let's start with the philosophical side of the coin. Philosophically, "newness" concerns an entity's origin and essence. "New" describes something that has not previously existed, as well as something that originates from its creative source. For example, for an idea to be considered new, it has to be the first of its kind, emanating from the mind of the person who conceived it. For an automobile to be considered new, it must not have been previously constructed or been available on the market; rather, it must have come directly from its manufacturer.

A BRAND-NEW ENTITY

In the same way, when the Bible utilizes the word *new*, it refers to something that has never before existed. It suggests that, as new creations, we are brand-new entities, the first of our kind. Doesn't that make you think about your life from a different perspective? When you realize what the Scriptures signify when they refer to you as being new in Christ, you must reexamine your life from that vantage point.

We often hear people say, in regard to their shortcomings, "God is working on me!" Yet, let me ask you this: when was the last time a brand-new car needed repair? When we think in those terms, either we have grossly misunderstood God's concept of new or there must be other factors at work.

MANY PEOPLE WHO HAVE CONFESSED CHRIST AND SINCERELY DESIRE TO HAVE AN INTIMATE RELATIONSHIP WITH HIM STILL DEAL WITH HABITUAL SIN, ADDICTIONS, GUILT, SHAME, AND CONDEMNATION FROM THE PAST. IN WHAT AREAS ARE YOU CURRENTLY STRUGGLING?

Many people who have confessed Christ as Savior and sincerely desire to have an intimate relationship with Him still deal with habitual sin, addictions, guilt, shame, and condemnation from the past. The question is, are these people new creations? If so, why are they still struggling? Well, theologically speaking, the moment a person is born again, they become a new creation. This newness is a spiritual reality, even though it may not be immediately demonstrated externally. For example, if a person who was an idol worshipper and had idolatrous tattoos on their skin gave their life to Jesus Christ, their tattoos would not automatically be erased. Even though they would be brand-new on the inside, they would not necessarily appear new externally, whether in their appearance or, to some extent, their behavior.

There is a difference between something being true ontologically, or in its nature, and that nature being manifested in practical ways. We will talk about the practical side of newness shortly, but for now, it is important to note the difference.

"OF A NEW KIND"

What does newness in the life of a believer look like? Second Corinthians 5:17 says, "*If any man be in Christ*, *he is a new creature* ["*creation*," NKJV]." Therefore, we know that the prerequisite for newness is "being in Christ." According to the Word of God, when we accept Jesus's lordship, a supernatural transformation happens within us. Once we are "*in Christ*," we can have the assurance that we are a "*new creation*."

The Greek word translated "*new*" in this verse is *kainos*, which means, in regard to form, something that is "recently made, fresh…unused"; and in terms of substance, "of a new kind." This gives me a picture of a baby coming into the world from its mother's womb. Everything about that newborn is fresh and brand-new. The Bible says it is the same way when we become new creations; we are fresh and vibrant. If we claim to be in Christ, there should be something profoundly new about our inner being because a regeneration has taken place within us.

In order to understand where our new life begins, we must know which aspect of our being becomes born again. Our spirit is what is born again; it is our spirit-man that becomes a new creation in Christ. From a New Testament perspective, the "spirit" refers to the vital force by which our bodies are animated. It is our essential being, our true self.

We were created in the image of God Himself. God is a triune Being—Father, Son, and Holy Spirit. Human beings are also tripartite in nature; we are a spirit that possesses a soul and lives in a body. When we are born again, our spirit-man unites with the Holy Spirit (the Spirit of Jesus Christ) and becomes one with Him. Paul writes, *"But he that is joined to the Lord is one spirit"* (1 Corinthians 6:17). Our innermost being is transformed into the image of Jesus Christ Himself. We mirror His very nature.

[We] *have put on the new man, which is renewed in knowledge after the image of Him that created him.* —Colossians 3:10

WHEN WE ARE IN CHRIST, THERE IS SOMETHING PROFOUNDLY NEW ABOUT OUR INNER BEING BECAUSE A REGENERATION HAS TAKEN PLACE WITHIN US.

The *"new man"* actually becomes like the One who created it. From our innermost being, or our spirit, we take on the thoughts, actions, and desires of God's Spirit. We are born from Him. This is a deep and profound truth because it means that the very essence and life of God the Father dwells in us. The *zoe* of God lives inside our born-again spirit. This transformation takes place supernaturally. It is much more than a mental exercise; it is, in fact, a miraculous mystery. Thus, to be born again means to become a new person with a new spiritual identity. We experience an inner transformation that transcends our feelings and emotions.

Some time ago, I purchased a complex and expensive computer, which came brand-new from the factory. It had a sealed, plastic covering over it, indicating it had never been used before. Since I was the first owner of this computer, I had to enter my own customized pass code to access it. Similarly, when we are born again, fresh from God's Spirit, we have our own spiritual access code. What is that code? It is the Word of God. It is through God's Word, and the Spirit's illumination of that Word to us, that we access all the benefits and features of our new life. Even though our spirit-man is a new creation, our body and soul are not yet renewed. They are still in a "used" condition. And this is the great challenge of the Christian experience—manifesting our newness of spirit in all areas of our life.

This is what I was referring to earlier about the difference between the ontological and the pragmatic. Our essence (spirit-man) is new and conformed to the image of Jesus Christ, but our soul and body are still alienated from the life of God's Spirit. How do we reconcile this discrepancy? We begin by understanding the terms *soul* and *body*.

 THE VERY ESSENCE AND LIFE OF GOD THE FATHER DWELLS IN US. THIS TAKES PLACE SUPERNATURALLY. IT IS MUCH MORE THAN A MENTAL EXERCISE; IT IS, IN FACT, A MIRACULOUS MYSTERY.

THE SOUL

The Greek word for "soul" is *psyche*, which means "the seat of the feelings, desires, affections, aversions (our heart, soul, etc.)." The word *soul* is sometimes used interchangeably with *spirit*, but for the purposes of this book, we will look at them as separate aspects of our being. The soul refers to our mind, will, and emotions. This is the place from which we make decisions.

In Matthew 5:28, Jesus said, *"But I say to you, That whosoever looks on a woman to lust after her has committed adultery with her already in his heart."* Although the Greek word for *"heart"* here is a different term than *psyche*, it can have essentially the same meaning, referring to "the fountain and seat of the thoughts, passions, desires, appetites, affections, purposes, endeavors." We can refer to this "fountain and seat" as the "soulish man." Jesus tells us that it is in a person's heart, or soul, that the decision to commit adultery is transacted. The same applies to all other decisions we make in regard to morality or other life choices.

THE BODY

The body refers to our physical faculties, including our eyes, ears, and mouth. The body carries out the affections and desires of the soul. If a person has not been born again, their spirit-man is still dead, their soul is enslaved to the devil and to ungodly passions, and their body is a conduit of sinful activity. But when we are born again, our spirit is filled with the life of God, and we can take authority over our soul and body. This means that our spirit can now direct our mind, will, and emotions, and our bodies can be conduits of righteousness.

However, in order for our redeemed nature to be reflected in our lives in practical ways, we have to appropriate our new nature through the power of the Holy Spirit. How do we do this? Remember that the access code to our new life is God's Word. Therefore, we begin by studying what our new life looks like so the Holy Spirit can teach and guide us in the truth. Since our spirit-man is made in the image of the One who created us, we need to invest time and energy to understand who the Creator is and what He is like. To really know God, we must not only read but also study and meditate on His Word. It is impossible to understand the new creation without having a knowledge of the Creator. And it is impossible to know the Creator without intimate knowledge of His Word. Surprisingly, those of us who call ourselves Christians do not spend nearly as much time as we should in God's Word.

The characteristics of our heavenly Father define for us the attributes we should display as His children. This is how we gauge how much of the new creation is being manifested in our lives. If we have been made new in Christ, our greatest desire is to please the Lord. Our lives are energized by the very life of God within us.

WHAT IS ULTIMATELY GUIDING YOUR LIFE DECISIONS— YOUR RENEWED SPIRIT OR YOUR SOUL?

When bad things happen to us that we cannot understand, we tend to blame them on God. When we do not have the marriage or the financial situation we want in life, we say, "It is not God's will!" I believe it is past time for such excuses. Often, the truth is that we have not really understood what it means to be new creations in Christ and receive all the provision and blessings He has for us through His Spirit, who lives within us.

Have you taken time to think about the fact that the life of the Almighty is resident inside your spirit? Religious tradition has taught many people that they are totally separate from God, and most church people behave as if that were the case. Yet, the truth is, we are not separate from God, but rather *"one spirit"* (1 Corinthians 6:17) with Him. The only way to walk in this spiritual reality is to believe what the Word of God says.

IT IS IMPOSSIBLE TO UNDERSTAND THE NEW CREATION WITHOUT HAVING A KNOWLEDGE OF THE CREATOR. AND IT IS IMPOSSIBLE TO KNOW THE CREATOR WITHOUT INTIMATE KNOWLEDGE OF HIS WORD.

THE LIFE OF THE SPIRIT

As believers, we are called to exemplify the life of the Spirit to the world around us. People should be able to look at us and tell that there is something unique about us. The transformation in which we invite others to partake should go beyond our churchgoing exteriors to a place deep within our true selves. Years ago, I was at a point in my life when I was going through all the motions of being a Christian and saying all the right things, but something was missing. I didn't understand why, as a Spirit-filled believer, I continued to struggle with feelings of loneliness and emptiness. I didn't know what it meant to truly be new. I read the Bible occasionally, and I went to church, but my life was not magnetized with the supernatural power of God. Let me clarify that when I say "supernatural power of God," I am not talking about having a onetime religious experience; I am referring to an ongoing relationship with God's Spirit that permanently transforms your life and impacts the lives of those around you. I knew there had to be more to the Christian life than what I was experiencing.

I was not conscious of the fact that I was a new creation because I was being told every Sunday how much of an "old creation" I was. There are pulpits across America where a message of depravity and condemnation is so enthusiastically proclaimed that neither the churchgoers nor the pastors themselves have any idea what it means to be new in Christ. It is as if the good news about the freedom of our new life has been forgotten and buried away in a dark cavern of religion. We may talk about repentance, exercising spiritual gifts, and serving others, but we omit the main ingredient of these aspects of the spiritual life. That essential quality is *newness*. It is the foundation of the life of the Spirit within us. Once we really understand this dynamic, we can understand everything that follows in our lives as believers.

You may be having—or have had—similar experiences. Many believers settle for a status quo of dissatisfaction with their spiritual lives. They see so many people around them who are also living beneath their potential as believers that they simply follow suit. I must tell you prophetically that Christ is not coming back for the status quo; He is coming back for a bride that is holy, "without spot and blemish." (See Ephesians 5:27.) He is coming for new creations!

I want to emphatically announce to you that if you have accepted Jesus Christ as your Lord and Savior by faith, you are in fact a new creation! Now is the time for you to start walking like it. Once you do, you will discover a world of unlimited supernatural possibilities. What if you could live every day of your life with joy? What if you knew how to defeat loneliness and depression? What if you could dwell in God's manifest presence for the rest of your life? What if you could walk in supernatural power to address the needs around you? All these benefits come when we fully grasp the mystery of our new nature in Christ.

 NEWNESS IS THE FOUNDATION OF THE LIFE OF THE SPIRIT WITHIN US.

VICTORY PRAYER

Father, I praise Your holy name for all that You are and all that You have done for me. Thank You that Your Spirit dwells within me. Thank You for empowering me to demonstrate the life of Christ to everyone around me. Thank You that Your supernatural life flows in and through me. I decree and declare that I am a conduit of divine activity. The world around me is shifted and molded by Your love operating through me. I have the victory in every area of my life. In Jesus's name, amen!

UNLOCKING THE CODE OF THE SUPERNATURAL INSIGHTS

1. What are the two main qualities of "newness"?

2. What is the prerequisite for spiritual newness?

3. Which part of our being becomes new in the new birth? Which parts need to be brought into alignment with God's nature?

4. What is the access code to our new life in the Spirit?

3

MORE THAN RELIGION

"For I say to you, That except your righteousness shall exceed the
righteousness of the scribes and Pharisees,
you shall in no case enter into the kingdom of heaven."
—Matthew 5:20

If I were to tell some people that being a Christian was much more than a religion, they would be puzzled. In fact, if I were to tell them that being a believer in Jesus Christ was not a religion at all, they would be very surprised. Yet comprehending and embracing the difference between religion and a relationship with Jesus completely changes our worldview and enables us to live as God intended us to.

"PACKAGING" GOD

To understand why, we need to define the word *religion*, which can be described as "a particular system of faith and worship." Religion is mankind's attempt to "package" God and His ways into a system that can be replicated and executed. When most people hear the word *religion*, they think of a set of regulations that one must follow to be found acceptable to the Creator. Religion is any effort on our part to please God through our performance.

There are many religions in the world, all with their own approaches to the deity of their choice and their own systems of worship. Some religions emphasize spiritual enlightenment. Others pursue the reconciliation of human relationships. Still others focus on the preservation of the earth. Using the general definition of "religion" mentioned above, we can see that being a believer in Christ does not necessarily fall under that category. Yes, there are tenets to the Christian faith, as well as practices of worship, and Christians may be involved in activities similar to those just mentioned. However, being a believer in Jesus Christ is so much more than that! The word *Christian* means "follower of Christ" or "imitator of Christ." This idea of being an imitator of someone encompasses not only following that person's actions, but also, in effect, taking on their nature.

WHEN WAS THE LAST TIME YOU THOUGHT OF

YOURSELF AS AN IMITATOR OF JESUS?

JESUS IMITATORS

And when he [Barnabas] had found him [Paul], he brought him to Antioch. And it came to pass, that a whole year they assembled themselves with the church, and taught many people. And the disciples were called Christians first in Antioch.   —Acts 11:26

The first time that believers in Christ were referred to as "Christians" was in the city of Antioch, in modern-day Turkey. This was a term that nonbelievers employed to articulate their perception of Jesus's followers. There was something about the believers in the early church that reminded everyone around them of Jesus Christ. In the same way that a son may remind people of his father, or a daughter her mother, we in the church should be expressions of Jesus and reminders to the world that He is alive. As we reflect Him, we become "Jesus imitators."

You can see how this idea goes far beyond the concept of religion. Being a Christian is a matter of identity, not ritual. The more conscious we are of this reality, the more successfully we will be positioned to live the Christian life. We are not commanded to complete a set of tasks that will please God, but we are commanded to allow Christ to live in and through us so that we can have a relationship with our heavenly Father and live in a way that pleases Him. In Galatians 2:20, Paul writes,

I am crucified with Christ: nevertheless I live; yet not I, but Christ lives in me: and the life which I now live in the flesh I live by the faith of the Son of God, who loved me, and gave Himself for me.

Paul declares that Christ is alive and active within him. It is not Paul's efforts at trying to attain to God's standards that are at work; it is the power of the Holy Spirit resident in Paul that enables him to become everything God intended him to be. Again, our life in Christ is so much more than a system of worship. It is a dynamic relationship with a living Jesus that changes every part of our lives. We cannot come to Christ by faith and remain the same people we were before. It is impossible! We need to grasp this simple but life-changing concept: following Jesus is not the same as following a list of dos and don'ts. Jesus is God incarnate who died on the cross for our sins to restore us to right fellowship with the Father and bring us to a place where the life of God could be made manifest in us.

 A DYNAMIC RELATIONSHIP WITH A LIVING JESUS CHANGES EVERY PART OF OUR LIVES.

In the Old Testament, God often manifested His presence to the Israelites in physical structures such as the tabernacle and temple, within the ark of the covenant. However, ever since Jesus's resurrection, God has dwelled in the spirit-man of the believer. We are the temple of the Holy Spirit! Paul talks about this truth in 1 Corinthians 6:19. Yet, in Galatians 2, he goes even further in expressing our connection and unity with God by asserting that, as a believer in Jesus, he is *"crucified with Christ."*

This statement expresses one of those ontological realities I mentioned earlier. Paul is saying that, in a spiritual sense, his old man (unregenerate nature) was nailed to the cross with Jesus and put to death once and for all. The former Paul is no more. He is dead! His new spirit-man is filled with Jesus Christ—so much so that Paul says he lives by the very faith of Christ. Not by faith *in* Christ but by the very faith *of* Christ! This faith is produced in us by God's Spirit. And that is what being a Christian is all about.

THE SECOND GREAT AWAKENING

In the early 1800s, there was a revival in American church culture that is known as the "Second Great Awakening." This was a time of dynamic preaching and great revival in many churches, which led to an emphasis on evangelism and missions. The Second Great Awakening shaped the very fabric of America. Thousands of people came to faith in Christ, and many charitable institutions and social-reform organizations were born. There was also a revisiting of biblical fundamentals. God mightily used many men and women to further His kingdom during this time.

However, I believe that an even greater awakening will occur in the church today once believers fully realize that being a Christian is not a religious exercise. Even with all of the awakenings that have occurred in church history, for the most part, the church still seems to omit, in teaching and practice, the simple truth of what it means for us to have a relationship with God as His new creations. We have failed to comprehend the very essence of our salvation.

God wants to awaken a deeper desire for Him within us. He wants us to know that being a Christian is not for "religious people" but for people who have failed, people who have been broken, people who need to be restored. This is very good news! It lets us know that we don't have to be "religious" to be able to walk in covenant relationship with God. (In fact, that would be impossible.) There is great spiritual power in relating to our heavenly Father on the basis of what Christ has done for us and not according to what we can accomplish on our own.

HOW MIGHT YOU BE TRYING TO LIVE YOUR CHRISTIAN LIFE IN A "RELIGIOUS" WAY?

RELIGION IS BASED ON WORKS

Religion is all about what we can do in our own ability. It is about how well we execute our tasks and how consistently we perform. However, trying to serve God in this way is a path to frustration and stagnation. Jesus is a living, breathing Person who makes His abode inside us. He is the One with the power to love God and live for Him. When we yield ourselves to this living, all-powerful Person, His very power is released in and through us!

The world doesn't need another religion; it has plenty already. What the world actually needs to see is the living Christ. When people see Him for who He really is, they will be drawn to Him with awe and wonder. Religion stands in the way of our ability to see God and to demonstrate Him to others.

Why is there such a strong temptation among people to be religious? Simple: human beings desire to be glorified. It is pride! Somewhere along the way, we were told that God is looking at our good behavior as a tool for measuring our faithfulness to Him. We think we will receive "points" if we can perform in the right way. In reality, God is not looking at our performance at all; He is looking at our new inner being, in which Christ dwells.

Religion is about "human doings," not about spiritual beings. I know firsthand the stranglehold that religion can have on someone's life. I was raised in a religious environment around religious people. For years, I wondered why I saw so many church people living defeated lives. This is not a criticism or a judgment against anyone, but it is just an observation. Seeing this state of affairs made me very confused about what my faith was really about. I saw people singing songs about God being the Healer, but they continued to be sick. I saw people testifying about God being their Provider, but they were enslaved to poverty. I saw people portray themselves as loving individuals while they were at church on a Sunday morning, but, in actuality, they were full of bitterness and resentment. To a young person growing up in the church, such contradictions sent mixed signals about the Christian faith.

Because they are ignorant of, or reject, the fact that being a Christian is not a religion, many people live disappointed and dissatisfied lives. The moment we attempt to package Christianity in the same box as every other religion, we make it appalling and off-putting. It is as distasteful as a police officer who takes bribes or a judge who is corrupt. It is only when we are functioning according to our purpose that we can truly reflect the love, grace, power, beauty, and holiness of God. If you don't believe me, try to fly with no technological assistance. You will quickly see that a human being is not a bird. We will never be birds. Similarly, Christianity will never be a religion. It was never intended to be! If we try to live as if it is, we will fail.

 THE WORLD DOESN'T NEED ANOTHER RELIGION; IT HAS PLENTY ALREADY. WHAT THE WORLD ACTUALLY NEEDS TO SEE IS THE LIVING CHRIST. WHEN PEOPLE SEE HIM FOR WHO HE REALLY IS, THEY WILL BE DRAWN TO HIM WITH AWE AND WONDER.

JESUS IS ALIVE!

That if you shall confess with your mouth the Lord Jesus, and shall believe in your heart that God has raised Him from the dead, you shall be saved. —Romans 10:9

Jesus is alive! We are not just following the sayings of a deceased religious leader, as the followers of most other religions are. Instead, we are engaging with the very fullness of the Godhead embodied in the person of Jesus Christ. This living Person dwells within us by virtue of the new birth. God has made us alive in Him. Religion doesn't give people life; it essentially kills them by leading them away from the true God or presenting expectations they can never live up to.

Please understand that there are positive aspects to almost every religion, but religions are not intended to make anyone alive. This is why, when we try to be religious in our attempts to follow Jesus, we enter into a rat race, a cycle that we find very difficult to get out of. We live a life of failure, frustration, and more failure. So many people today are unnecessarily battling depression and defeat because they don't know that Jesus has already paid the price for their sin and human weaknesses. They don't realize that to be a believer means to have the very life of God operating within them, and that this spiritual life is able to effect change in every area of their lives.

 WE ARE NOT JUST FOLLOWING THE SAYINGS OF A DECEASED RELIGIOUS LEADER, AS THE FOLLOWERS OF MOST OTHER RELIGIONS ARE. INSTEAD, WE ARE ENGAGING WITH THE VERY FULLNESS OF THE GODHEAD EMBODIED IN THE PERSON OF JESUS CHRIST.

The Holy Spirit has the power to quicken us, or make us alive, and give us a high quality of life that we cannot even fathom. Oh, what a mystery!

Sometimes, it is hard for us to admit that we are in a place where we are dissatisfied with our Christian life. A place where going to church is not yielding the results we desire. A place where our attempts to be morally good are not working. A place where we say things like, "God, I will never do *that* again!" yet find ourselves doing it again and again. Jesus did not come to make us religious. He came to make us alive! The moment we accept this simple truth, we enter into a new reality—a reality of victory.

VICTORY PRAYER

Father, I thank You that Your Word is the final authority in my life. I acknowledge the truth that You are alive within me. I thank You that my righteousness is not based on religious works, but instead on what Jesus Christ accomplished in His death and resurrection. I confess that Jesus is the Lord of my life. All of my validation, worth, and acceptance comes from Him. From this day forward, I walk in the power of the Holy Spirit. I am not controlled by religion, but I am free to serve You in truth. In Jesus's name, amen!

UNLOCKING THE CODE OF THE SUPERNATURAL INSIGHTS

1. What are some characteristics of religion?

2. How does our new life in Christ differ from religion?

3. What does Galatians 2:20 teach us about how we are meant to live our lives in Christ?

4. Why is there such a strong temptation among people to be religious? Where does performance-based religion lead us?

MIRACLE TESTIMONY

SUPERNATURALLY SAVED FROM DEATH

A family friend who lives in Africa was walking on the side of the road in the northern part of his country, which is heavily populated by radical Muslims. The Muslims had been on a campaign of violence for many months. They were terrorizing villages, killing women and children and burning homes to ashes while the inhabitants were still inside. As this man walked along, he witnessed Christians being impaled. Before he could run the other way, the Muslims caught him and held him down so they could pierce him with a rod. Under his breath, the man called on Jesus. There was a sudden blast from heaven that sounded like a trumpet. Apparently, this was a language that only the Muslims could understand because they immediately threw down their rods and ran away. The man's life was supernaturally saved. Jesus is not merely a storybook character. He is alive and all-powerful—and He lives in you.

4

YOU MUST BE BORN AGAIN!

"Jesus answered and said to him, Verily, verily, I say to you, Except a man be born again, he cannot see the kingdom of God."
—John 3:3

In the early 1990s, the "seeker-friendly" movement emerged in the American church. This movement was aimed at creating an atmosphere where nonbelievers would feel comfortable going to church and be able to relate to the messages that were presented. Pastors everywhere were encouraged to exchange their suits and ties or other "pious-looking" apparel for a more trendy, relevant look. "Offensive" materials were removed from the sanctuary, and the length of services was shortened. This was the dawn of the modern church, the effects of which we are still seeing today.

Although there were many positive aspects to this reshaping of church culture, unfortunately, some essential elements were lost in translation. In my opinion, the seeker-friendly movement has created a kind of spiritual narcissism, where people are more concerned about their church buildings than they are about the kingdom of God. While there has been a strong focus on church involvement and family engagement, not enough attention has been given to empowering people with the Word of God—especially in regard to teaching people what it means to be a new creation in Christ. The result has been a generational and cultural shift in the church. Just as the modern family phenomenon has an external appearance of functionality that masks its internal flaws, so the church has developed an external shell of functionality that covers up its serious internal weaknesses.

We live in an age when many people place great emphasis on looking the part of a Christian, and little emphasis on truly being born again. One of the questions we are exploring in this book is, if hundreds of thousands of people attend church on a regular basis, why do so many of them still live defeated lives? If numbers of people identify themselves as Christians, why are we not seeing the impact on the world around us that we saw in the early church? I believe it is because people do not know who they are.

WE LIVE IN AN AGE WHEN MANY PEOPLE PLACE GREAT EMPHASIS ON LOOKING THE PART OF A CHRISTIAN, AND LITTLE EMPHASIS ON TRULY BEING BORN AGAIN.

UNRAVELING THE MYSTERY

In the gospel of John, Jesus has an intriguing and powerful conversation with Nicodemus, a prominent religious leader of the day. Nicodemus goes to Jesus at night and acknowledges that He has been sent by God. Jesus replies with a profound statement—He emphatically declares than unless someone is *"born again,"* that person cannot see the kingdom of God.

If you grew up in a Christian setting, the term *born again* is probably familiar to you, especially if you have been around evangelical or charismatic circles for some time. However, Nicodemus could not understand what Jesus was talking about because, apparently, all he had ever experienced was religion. All he had ever known was going through the motions and performing to earn God's love. We can only imagine what Nicodemus was thinking when Jesus made that declaration. But we do know his response: *"Nicodemus says to Him, How can a man be born when he is old? can he enter the second time into his mother's womb, and be born?"* (John 3:4).

As we can see, Jesus had gone way over Nicodemus's head with this whole born-again idea. We may need to admit that it has often gone over our heads, too. Yet, Jesus's response provides the keys to unraveling the mystery of our new nature. It contains the foundational truths we must understand in order to experience the fullness of what the Father has given us. And, more specifically, it explains how we are able to experience God's supernatural kingdom.

Jesus answered Nicodemus's question in this way: *"Verily, verily, I say to you, Except a man be born of water and of the Spirit, he cannot enter into the kingdom of God. That which is born of the flesh is flesh; and that which is born of the Spirit is spirit"* (John 3:5–6). What did Jesus mean when He said we must be born of water and the Spirit? He was not speaking of simple water baptism here. The harmony of Scripture reveals that water baptism, in itself, does not have a redemptive capacity.

Nicodemus had asked Jesus how someone could enter into their mother's womb a second time to be born. Why did he ask this question? Well, the first reason is that, in the natural realm, this is exactly what it means to be born. The Greek word translated *"born"* in this passage is *gennao*, which means "to be begotten" or "to be fathered." Babies are seeded by their natural fathers and born into this world through their mothers' wombs. They are literally carried in a sack of amniotic fluid until they are delivered. This process was the only orientation Nicodemus had regarding birth. Therefore, to him, being "born again" would require another physical entrance into the world.

The New Testament record of Jesus's reply combines two Greek words with the conjunction *kai*, which is translated as "and" in English. Jesus said that a man not only needs to be born naturally, but he (indeed also) must be born from the Spirit of God. A natural birth alone does not qualify you for God's kingdom; you must have a spiritual birth.

I believe the second reason Nicodemus asked this question is because his life lacked spirituality. The notion of a person being reborn did not fit into his performance-based paradigm. It is easy to be critical of Nicodemus for being ignorant and religious-oriented, but there are many people in the body of Christ today who still do not understand what being born again means for them. Countless people who call themselves Christians are simply going through the religious motions they have been taught. Yet, when we accept the salvation and lordship of Jesus Christ by faith, in that instant, we become children of God. We were already children by virtue of our creation, but once we receive Jesus into our hearts, we are God's sons and daughters.

HEAVENLY DNA

It is the Holy Spirit who births us into God's kingdom. As I described earlier, we now have the DNA of our heavenly Father written in our spirit-man. This is why Jesus said, *"That which is born of the flesh is flesh; and that which is born of the Spirit is spirit."* What you are born of determines your nature. Due to the fall of mankind, our physical birth made us carnal in nature, but our spiritual rebirth makes us spiritual in nature.

Generally speaking, an individual's nature can be defined as the complex emotional and intellectual attributes that determine their characteristic actions and reactions. Thus, our nature determines how we function; it determines our actions, which arise from our innermost desires. This is why people in the world cannot really understand spiritual matters. Such matters cannot be taught—they must be revealed to us by the Holy Spirit. As we have been discussing, we cannot walk out the Christian life without having a brand-new nature that the Spirit of God produces in us. John 1:12–13 says:

> But as many as received Him [Jesus], to them gave He **power to become the sons of God**, even to them that believe on His name: which were born, not of blood, nor of the will of the flesh, nor of the will of man, but of God.

Our spiritual birth takes place the moment we repent of our sins and accept Christ as Lord. John declares that those who receive Jesus Christ are empowered to become *"sons of God."* The Greek word translated *"become"* is *ginomai*, which means "to come into existence." This is the same word we looked at earlier from John 1:3 that is rendered as *"made"*: *"All things were made by Him; and without Him was not any thing made that was made."*

The apostle John tells us that the new birth is not based on the flesh or on the will of man, but on God alone. We see again that we are not saved by shear willpower. Our lives are not spiritually transformed by human effort. We can become new only through the power of God's Spirit. It is not our denominational affiliation or our moral code that makes us successful in the Christian life; it is being born of the Spirit of God and living according to that new birth. Only when we are born of the Spirit can we walk out the Christian experience.

Have you ever seen a mother give her newborn child a training manual on how to eat or walk? Of course not. Why? The potential and ability for eating and walking is already inside the child's genetic code. In time, what is wired into that child's very DNA will come to manifestation. In the same manner, when we are truly born again, we do not need to be taught to love or obey God. It is already wired within us by virtue of the new birth. All that we need to do now is to be conformed to the image of God that is within us.

WHAT DOES BEING BORN AGAIN MEAN TO YOU?

If you are still in love with living a sinful lifestyle, without restraint or remorse for wrongdoing, then I would say you need to be born again. You must understand that a born-again spirit desires to please God all the time. Therefore, what we often call "conviction" of wrongdoing is essentially a disagreement between our spirit and our flesh. Our inner man is in perfect fellowship and alignment with our heavenly Father. From the very core of our being, we want to obey God. We want to walk in His ways and fulfill what He has called us to do on this earth. We have an internal abhorrence of sin and anything that defies God. Having this inner nature is what it means to be born again.

WHEN WE ARE A NEW CREATION, FROM THE VERY CORE OF OUR BEING, WE WANT TO PLEASE GOD!

ONE WITH THE FATHER

In John 10:30, Jesus said, *"I and My Father are one."* This is a great mystery. How is Jesus one with the Father? In Hebrew culture, a son was considered the same as his father. When Jesus used this Jewish idiom, the Pharisees wanted to stone Him because He was implying He was equal with God. In the minds of the Pharisees, Jesus was committing blasphemy by suggesting that He was God's offspring.

Jesus responded to the Pharisees by challenging them with the Scriptures: *"Is it not written in your law, I said, You are gods?"* (John 10:34). Jesus was quoting Psalm 82:6: *"I have said, You are gods; and all of you are children of the Most High."* It seemed impossible for the Pharisees to fathom this reality. How could we identity ourselves with God? However, if God called the children of Israel "gods," then how could it be hard to fathom that Jesus was the Son of God? Simple! Religion and tradition had taught them that God was distant from them. He was a mere concept, not a living, loving Father who desires to reveal Himself to us.

It seems that many people today are terrified to embrace the fact that they are one with God. Being in Christ should remove our fear, guilt, and sense of unworthiness before the Lord. Yet religion still suggests to us that we are necessarily distant from Him.

How do we know that, when we are born again, we are one with God? After declaring in John 10:30 that He and the Father are one, Jesus prayed this prayer to the heavenly Father: *"That they all may be one; as You, Father, are in Me, and I in You, that they also may be one in Us: that the world may believe that You have sent Me"* (John 17:21). We are one with the Father because we are one with Christ, and Christ is one with the Father.

Remember that the Scriptures tell us, *"But he that is joined to the Lord is **one spirit**"* (1 Corinthians 6:17). Wow! We are one spirit with the Father. He dwells in us, and we dwell in Him. This is such an awesome truth that it has the potential to rock our world. When we see God as much more than a distant deity who has given us a to-do list, when we see Him as our loving and infinitely powerful Father, our lives will be permanently altered.

Can you comprehend what this truth implies? You are one with the very Creator of the universe! You no longer need to consider life something to battle through. Instead, you can approach life from a position of spiritual power and authority. When depression rears its ugly head in your life or in the life of a loved one, you can open your mouth and declare that you and the Father are one! All of His love and provision is available to you.

HOW DOES KNOWING THAT YOU ARE ONE SPIRIT WITH GOD CHANGE YOUR PERSPECTIVE OF YOUR RELATIONSHIP WITH HIM?

LIBERATED FROM BONDAGE

Why are we so afraid to accept what the Bible says? Once we receive what God's Word declares about us, it will remove excuses from our thinking and our vocabulary—excuses that cause our lives to remain far below what they are meant to be. When we embrace the truth that the same Spirit who raised Jesus from the dead dwells inside of us, victory will be ours for the taking.

In my church, we have seen people liberated from all types of bondage as they have simply received this message I am sharing with you. We explain the Word of God and remind them that they are new creations in Christ Jesus. The enemy hates this way of thinking because it undermines his power in the lives of believers. You must understand that Satan draws his power from guilt, shame, and condemnation. In contrast, as Christians, we draw our power and authority from our secure identity in Christ. The more we know who we are—and whose we are—the more authority we will exercise over the kingdom of darkness.

LIVING WATER

New life flows within us, and new life flows from us. In John 4:14, Jesus said that a well of living water would spring up inside us *"into everlasting life."* This living water causes us never to lack spiritual refreshing and power! In John 4, the Samaritan woman with whom Jesus spoke was invited to experience this spiritual water. Jesus knew that her life was an absolute mess. He also knew that the solution to her deepest needs was not physical water from Jacob's well—it was His living water. Where does this water come from? It comes from the Holy Spirit. When we accept Christ into our spirits, we become filled with God's life-giving presence.

The Samaritan woman caught on to this revelation, and she was forever changed by the power of God. She was now in a position to confidently proclaim that her life had been transformed and to lead others to this living water. In John 4:24, Jesus says, *"God is a Spirit: and they that worship Him must worship Him in spirit and in truth."* That is the essence of true worship. How can people worship God fully if they are not born again? The answer is, they cannot! It is impossible to connect with God as your Source if your spirit does not identify with Him as your Father.

We must be born again by God's Spirit so that we can walk as the Spirit-breathed sons and daughters we were destined to be. Again, when someone is born again, they desire, from their innermost being, to please and serve God with all that is in them. This desire does not need to be pumped or primed by religion or a particular church's methods or procedures; rather, it is an internal desire that propels every aspect of their life and worship. It is more than an emotional response to the prompting of a preacher; it is a spiritual response to the prompting of the Holy Spirit.

God neither wants to beat you down with religion nor stroke your existential ego. He simply wants you to know who you are in Him. From this knowledge, you will receive a much-needed shift in your spiritual paradigm. Imagine living in such victory that you never even get a chance to invite people to church because they are already too busy asking if they can attend with you. Imagine the supernatural power of God flowing through you in such a way that people are healed and delivered when you walk by their cubicles at work. These are not lofty ideas; this is the reality of living as a born-again, Spirit-filled believer in Jesus Christ.

> OUR DESIRE TO PLEASE AND SERVE GOD IS AN INTERNAL YEARNING THAT PROPELS EVERY ASPECT OF OUR LIFE AND WORSHIP. IT IS MORE THAN AN EMOTIONAL RESPONSE TO THE PROMPTING OF A PREACHER; IT IS A SPIRITUAL RESPONSE TO THE PROMPTING OF THE HOLY SPIRIT.

VICTORY PRAYER

Father, in the name of Jesus Christ, I thank You for who You are and all that You have done for me. Today, I accept the truth that I am one spirit with You. According to John 10:30 and John 17:21, I am one with Jesus, as He is one with the Father. Right now, I submit myself to the lordship of Christ. I declare that I am born again of incorruptible seed. The Holy Spirit has given me spiritual birth, and I have Your DNA within my being. Thank You, Father, for revealing this mystery to me! In Jesus's name, amen!

UNLOCKING THE CODE OF THE SUPERNATURAL INSIGHTS

1. Name some problems with the "seeker-friendly" approach of the modern church.

2. What ultimately determines our nature?

3. What does a born-again spirit continually desire?

4. What does it mean to be one with the Father?

5

CONSEQUENCES OF THE RELIGIOUS SPIRIT

"If any man among you seem to be religious, and bridles not his tongue, but deceives his own heart, this man's religion is vain. Pure religion and undefiled before God and the Father is this, To visit the fatherless and widows in their affliction, and to keep himself unspotted from the world."
—James 1:26–27

While I was growing up in a very religious environment, I saw people perform for God rather than love Him. I saw young people my age opt for living according to the world instead of living for the Lord, even though many of their parents were leaders in the church. Although I did not fully understand the implications of what was occurring, God was trying to show me the difference between being religious and being a Christian. He wanted me to understand the distinction between a man-made religious system and a God-ordained relationship.

PURE RELIGION

The Holy Spirit began to open my eyes to the deep revelation in James 1 that God was calling me to apply to my life. We need to understand that the apostle James's reference to *"religion"* in verse 26 is not used in the way we have been discussing so far—a works-oriented performance to gain God's approval. It simply refers to a system of worship. James actually uses the term *"pure religion."* This must mean that there can be "pure religion" and "defiled religion." The word *"pure"* here signifies "clean." In an ethical sense, the term means "free from corrupt desire, from sin and guilt" or "free from every admixture of what is false, sincere; genuine." To practice defiled religion is to perform religious rituals out of incorrect or corrupt motives. To practice pure religion is to exercise spiritual disciplines from the right motives.

James examines three qualities of those who practice pure religion. The first quality is control over one's tongue. One aspect of the fruit of the Spirit is *"self-control"* (Galatians 5:23 NKJV). What we say comes from what is in our hearts, and our mouths often betray what we really believe. As Jesus said, *"For of the abundance of the heart* [a person's] *mouth speaks"* (Luke 6:45). We must allow the Holy Spirit to direct all that we say and do.

DO YOU HAVE THE QUALITIES OF SOMEONE WHO

PRACTICES "PURE RELIGION"?

The second characteristic of someone who practices pure religion is that they actively care for *"the fatherless and widows"* (James 1:27). Typically, in New Testament days, those who were widows and orphans were poor, so James is talking about the way we treat people who are socially and economically oppressed. I personally believe he is not just speaking of those who are widows and orphans in a physical sense, but also of those who are widows and orphans in a spiritual or emotional sense. This means that the church has a God-ordained responsibility to reach beyond our comfort zones and extend ourselves to help those in need.

The third qualification of people whose religion is pure is that they keep themselves *"unspotted from the world"* (verse 27). What does this mean? The Greek word translated *"unspotted"* is *aspilos*, which can signify "free from censure, irreproachable." Thus, we are expected to live lives that are above reproach and separated from the world system, which refers to ways of thinking and behaving that are contrary to God's ways.

According to this passage from James, if our religious experience does not include these three characteristics, it is *"vain"* (verse 26). The Greek word for this term is *mataios*, meaning "devoid of force, truth, success, result" or "useless, of no purpose."

> THE CHURCH HAS A GOD-ORDAINED RESPONSIBILITY TO REACH BEYOND OUR COMFORT ZONES AND EXTEND OURSELVES TO HELP THOSE IN NEED.

VAIN RELIGION

In my travels throughout the United States, I talk to many different kinds of people, and I always ask them this question: "Do you have a relationship with God?" The answer I receive most frequently is, "I am not religious; I am spiritual!" You may have heard other people make this statement. What do they imply by it? Are they referring to the qualifications set forth in James 1:26–27? Many of these people may follow a certain system of worship, but it is not one that lines up with the Word of God. The issue is not a matter of terminology, but whether their religion or spirituality is vain. If they are not submitted to the lordship of Jesus, demonstrating His character, then their system of worship is void of power and useless. Even though they might not attend church regularly or consider themselves religious, they are still guilty of having "vain religion."

What is the culprit behind the "I am not religious" mindset? Why do people aggressively assert their so-called spirituality when you ask them about their relationship with God? There is something called a "religious spirit," and it is prevalent in American culture at large and in the church in particular. A religious spirit may stem from a sinful, fleshly attitude or a demonic influence—or both. This spirit promotes religious activity void of supernatural power and true spiritual, physical, and emotional transformation. It causes people to say one thing and do another. This spirit tries to mingle the things of God with the things of this world. If a person has a religious spirit, they may claim to be a "good person" even though their heart is full of darkness.

Remember what James said: if our religion is not characterized by exercising self-control, reaching out to those who are socially and economically oppressed, and keeping ourselves unspotted from the world, it is vain.

ONLY A FORM OF GODLINESS

The apostle Paul writes in 2 Timothy 3:1–5:

*This know also, that in the last days perilous times shall come. For men shall be lovers of their own selves, covetous, boasters, proud, blasphemers, disobedient to parents, unthankful, unholy, without natural affection, trucebreakers, false accusers, incontinent [without self-control], fierce, despisers of those that are good, traitors, heady, high-minded, lovers of pleasures more than lovers of God; **having a form of godliness, but denying the power thereof**: from such turn away.*

What does Paul mean by the phrase "*having a form of godliness, but denying the power thereof*"? The Greek word translated "*godliness*" is *eusebeia*, one meaning of which is "piety toward God." The Greek word for "*power*" is *dynamis*, which refers to explosive power. In these last days, people will succumb to a demonic religious spirit that will be released in the earth. They will look pious, but they will have no power for real change—for themselves or others. This condition will cause people to go through the motions of seeking God while actually rejecting Him.

I can identify with such a condition because I was included in this category for a period of my life. For many years, I believed that merely going to church was sufficient, and I was surrounded by people who felt the same way. They thought that if they participated in religious activity, they were right with God. Beloved, this is a deadly way of thinking. It is vital for us to have a genuine, ongoing, supernatural relationship with the Lord.

Moreover, Paul says that in the last days, there will be people who are so in love with themselves that they will gratify their flesh at all costs. They will be blasphemers of what is holy. They will despise believers who exhibit the goodness of the Lord. Yet, many of these individuals will also be actively involved in their local churches! Today, such behavior is already common in the church as a whole.

HOW RESPONSIVE ARE YOU TO GOD'S WORD AND SPIRIT?

The religious spirit encourages people to sound like believers but not *be* believers. It seeks to prohibit people from being changed on the inside. This spirit is the impetus for much of the performance-based Christianity that we see today. When people have a lack of genuine spiritual power in their lives, it is no wonder that we see problems like teenage pregnancy and drug use among church members.

One study showed that among young adults aged eighteen to twenty-nine who have a Christian background, only 10 percent are "resilient disciples," in contrast to those who are merely "habitual churchgoers," "nomads, or lapsed Christians," or "prodigals, or ex-Christians."[1] When I was growing up, a number of the youth who sung in the choir and were involved in various ministries in the church possessed absolutely no love for God. Many of their parents were content with their simply going to church. I can count on one hand the number of young people I grew up with who are in full-time ministry today. I believe that this result—reflected in many other churches, as well—is due to the fact that the church has, in many ways, denied the power of God in favor of religious performance. We who are born again are supposed to keep ourselves unspotted from the world. We who are born again are meant to be responsive to God's Word and Spirit, through which we can experience real transformation.

God is not interested in our church participation if our heart is not in the right place. He is interested in what James referred to as *"true religion."* False, or vain, religion only produces spiritual barrenness.

THE MESSAGE OF THE FIG TREE

A passage in the gospel of Mark gives us deep insight into the religious spirit. Jesus is about to complete His earthly ministry by going to the cross. His death is the fulfillment of messianic prophecy, much of which is found in the book of Isaiah. Earlier, Jesus had experienced His triumphal entry into Jerusalem, where He was met with praise and laudation from many of the Jewish people. This was a very critical time in Jesus's life that deserves our serious attention because every act He carries out from this point on

---

1. "Only 10% of Christian Twentysomethings Have Resilient Faith," Barna Group, September 24, 2019, https://www.barna.com/research/of-the-four-exile-groups-only-10-are-resilient-disciples.

lays the groundwork for how His disciples are to live once He leaves the earthly realm.

And Jesus entered into Jerusalem, and into the temple: and when He had looked round about upon all things, and now the evening was come, He went out to Bethany with the twelve. And on the morrow, when they were come from Bethany, He was hungry: and seeing a fig tree afar off having leaves, He came, if haply He might find any thing thereon: and when He came to it, He found nothing but leaves; for the time of figs was not yet. And Jesus answered and said to it, No man eat fruit of you hereafter for ever. And His disciples heard it.

—Mark 11:11–14

As Jesus traveled from Bethany, He was hungry, so He searched for a source of satisfaction. To His excitement, He saw a fig tree. Unfortunately, when He came close to the fig tree, He saw that there was nothing on it but leaves because it wasn't yet the season for figs. Jesus responded to this situation by cursing the fig tree. He declared that no one would ever eat fruit from that particular tree ever again. The next day, the disciples saw that the tree that Jesus had cursed had withered and died. (See verse 20.)

Why would Jesus curse this fig tree? Clearly, the tree was out of season! Shouldn't He have understood this natural phenomenon? In order to gain a better understanding of this passage, we must examine the prophetic implications of Jesus's journey to Jerusalem. Earlier in Mark 11, the people had declared, *"Hosanna; blessed is he that comes in the name of the Lord: Blessed be the kingdom of our father David, that comes in the name of the Lord: Hosanna in the highest"* (verses 9–10). This was a messianic proclamation because the Messiah was to sit on the throne of David.

This event is important because Jesus was functioning as the King of Kings and exercising kingdom authority. Then, the next morning, He came to the fruitless fig tree. As I began to pray about this passage, God showed me that Jesus was not cursing the natural tree itself, but He was actually cursing the spirit of religion among the leaders and people in Jerusalem. The leaders did not accept that He was the Messiah and even plotted

His death. And many of the same people who had worshipped Jesus in Jerusalem were calling for His crucifixion later in the week.

The fig tree is an important biblical symbol. In Genesis 3:7, after their fall, Adam and Eve sewed fig leaves together in order to make garments to cover themselves. Their action is an example of mankind's shallow efforts to hide its sin and shame, to cover itself apart from God. The fig tree is a perfect symbol for religion. From a distance, the tree looked adequate, but on closer inspection, its true condition could be seen: it was all form and no substance. God wants us to be very aware of His indictment against the religious spirit, which fought against Jesus during His entire earthly ministry and continues to war against the true church today.

Let's now look at the characteristics of the spirit of religion, which exhibits the qualities revealed in the illustration of the fig tree.

SPIRITUAL BARRENNESS

The first attribute of the fig tree that Jesus cursed was barrenness. A religious spirit is incapable of producing any real fruit. It is responsible for most, if not all, fruitlessness in the lives of born-again believers. Religion drains our spiritual fervor and passion for Jesus. It causes us to focus on ourselves and our own strength and ability. Thus, the Lord cursed the fig tree because it represented the spirit that fights against God's kingdom plan of redemption, growth, and multiplication. It is a counterfeit of true change and transformation.

I am concerned that the church has been seduced by a religious spirit that seeks to draw people into a vicious cycle of striving for God's love and acceptance while not being able to produce lasting fruit of the Spirit. Religious people never reproduce themselves as true believers; they are incapable of making disciples of Jesus. One of God's first commandments to Adam and Eve was, *"Be fruitful, and multiply, and replenish the earth, and subdue it"* (Genesis 1:28). Yet the spirit of religion is narcissistic in nature, focused mainly on religious tradition and denominations. It prevents personal spiritual growth and maturity. People who live according to this spirit may attend church regularly, but they will never invite others to church because, for them, church is not a transformational experience; it is simply a ritual.

Thus, the spirit of religion is responsible for a lack of quantitative and qualitative growth in local churches. Believers' spiritual barrenness prevents them from developing a heart for the lost and a desire to see those in the world won to the Lord. It will not allow them to really rejoice when a sinner comes to repentance because, in their minds, repentance does not have any real value. The religious spirit also prevents people from seeing beyond the four walls of their church to the needs of the world around them. It disables them from taking spiritual dominion over cities, states, countries, and nations.

The religious mindset is completely the opposite of God's original purpose and plan. He intended that every union He sanctioned would produce fruit. For example, in the natural course of life, when a husband and wife come together in covenant consummation, a baby is conceived. Why? Because humanity is meant to multiply, and the family is an institution of God. Similarly, our union with Jesus Christ is supposed to produce spiritual fruit. Spiritual barrenness is like physical impotency; no matter how much effort is put forth, there is no fruit.

Christians everywhere have been called by God to be fruitful and multiply in all areas of their lives. Jesus said, *"Herein is My Father glorified, that you bear much fruit; so shall you be My disciples"* (John 15:8). Spiritual fruit is produced in our lives when we are intimate with Jesus Christ. As you can imagine, the religious spirit resists true intimacy with the Lord and fellowship with other believers in the church. Those who are bound by a religious spirit find it difficult to pray, fast, worship, read the Bible, or share their faith with passion and sincerity. Many people are frustrated because they are trying hard to serve the Lord to the best of their knowledge, but they are not producing the results they read about in the Bible. The barren fig tree of religion is largely responsible for this widespread condition.

SPIRITUAL FRUIT IS PRODUCED IN OUR LIVES WHEN WE ARE INTIMATE WITH JESUS CHRIST.

HYPOCRISY

Another attribute of the fig tree that Jesus cursed is hypocrisy. In ancient Greek and Roman culture, a stage actor who wore a mask to entertain spectators was called *hypokrites*, the term from which we derive the word *hypocrite*. Attached to the mask was a mechanical device that amplified the person's voice. Through this device, an actor was able to project a different sound than his real voice. This is a fitting description of what is taking place in the church today. In simple terms, a religious hypocrite is someone who puts on a mask and "voice" of religiosity while they are around other church people, but once they are alone, they remove their mask and live according to their true nature.

The religious spirit is marked by chronic hypocrisy. Like the fig tree that Jesus cursed in Mark 11, the hypocritical spirit of religion creates an illusion of fruitfulness, but upon closer examination, is shown to have produced nothing but leaves. As I mentioned previously, fig leaves represent mankind's inadequate covering for sin.

One of the biggest complaints that I hear from non-believers about the church is that Christians are hypocrites. Now, I am aware that as we are growing in our faith, we will all face challenges with temptation and sin. I am not saying that committing a sin makes someone a hypocrite, and this is probably not what unbelievers are referring to either. The hypocrisy I am referring to is an intentional performance put on by someone who does not currently have an authentic relationship with Jesus—whether that person has received Christ or not.

Many people in the church live much different lives from Monday through Friday than they do on Sunday. During my freshman year of college, I witnessed students drinking, smoking, and going off to have sex outside of marriage on Saturday night, and then singing in the choir at chapel service on Sunday morning. I was confused by this behavior because I would see them doing the same thing every weekend. Hypocrisy always causes a person to engage in religious performance without real change. Every time we hear the Word of God, it is supposed to transform us on the inside. The spirit of religion does not want change to take place in people's lives, so it keeps them trapped in a cycle of pretension and hypocrisy.

All hypocrisy is not as extreme as the previous examples, but it is just as deadly to us spiritually if it goes unchecked. It may come in the form of talking about God being first in our lives without having a personal relationship with Him that validates that claim. It may be as simple as functioning in a ministry role or office without having the necessary holy lifestyle to qualify for that position. Like a cancer, hypocrisy eats away at the fabric of church culture. The spirit of religion seeks to rob the body of Christ of its witness and authority. Beloved, Jesus does not want us to be hypocrites but to be genuine believers who manifest His love and power in the earth.

DECEPTION

Hypocrisy opens the door to deception—of ourselves and others. The Bible states, *"But be you doers of the word, and not hearers only, deceiving your own selves"* (James 1:22). James says that if we develop a habit of hearing the Word without doing the Word, we will become deceived. The Greek word rendered *"deceiving"* in this verse is *paralogizomai*, which can mean "to reckon wrong, miscount" or "to cheat (or deceive) by false reckoning." If we don't act on the Word that we hear or read, it will cause us to calculate incorrectly. We will miscount and misinterpret our own spiritual maturity—or lack thereof. This is a very dangerous condition! If we attribute spiritual attributes to ourselves that we do not actually possess, we are deceived.

Suppose someone who is not a police officer wore a law enforcement uniform every day. Eventually, they might begin to believe they were a real police officer. But if a real crime took place that people expected them to respond to, they would be unable to act with the authority their uniform suggests. Someone might call out to them, saying, "Help, officer, this man is trying to mug me! Arrest him!" The impersonator would not have the training or authority to help. While this person looked the part of a police officer, they had no substance to back it up.

The Bible gives an account of the sons of Sceva who tried to cast out a demon in the name of *"Jesus whom Paul preaches"* (Acts 19:13). The demon responded by saying, *"Jesus I know, and Paul I know, but who are you?"* (verse 15). The man who was demon-possessed ended up beating up the sons of

Sceva, leaving them to flee *"naked and wounded"* (verse 16). Talk about a deliverance session gone wrong! These men thought they had a religious formula for casting out demons, but they didn't have the relationship with Jesus or the spiritual authority to deal with demonic possession.

James says, *"If any be a hearer of the word, and not a doer, he is like to a man beholding his natural face in a glass: for he beholds himself, and goes his way, and immediately forgets what manner of man he was"* (James 1:23–24). When we fail to obey the Word, it is as if we have looked in a mirror and then promptly forgotten the image of ourselves that we saw. The Greek word for *"forgets"* in this passage is *epilanthanomai*, which, in addition to meaning "to forget," can also signify "neglecting, no longer caring for." If we fail to regularly look at ourselves in a mirror, we may become careless about our appearance and become unpresentable. The "forgetting" James mentions in verse 24 refers to spiritual carelessness.

He goes on to say, *"But whoso looks into the perfect law of liberty, and continues therein, he being not a forgetful hearer, but a doer of the work, this man shall be blessed in his deed"* (verse 25). This verse reinforces the fact that the mirror is, indeed, the Word of God, *"the perfect law of liberty."* Most mirrors simply reflect reality. Therefore, we gaze into the Word in order to see our true spiritual state. As we continue to read, study, and meditate on God's Word, we shine His light on the areas of our lives that need to be transformed. Once we obey the Word regarding those areas, we will experience freedom. The evidence that a person is under the influence of a spirit of deception is that they quote the Scriptures while experiencing absolutely no freedom in their lives.

We can see how the religious spirit produces only barrenness, hypocrisy, and deception. As I mentioned earlier, this deception may not be limited to ourselves. The outward form of religion in our lives may deceive others into thinking the Christian life is all ritual and form, without substance.

 AS WE CONTINUE TO READ, STUDY, AND MEDITATE ON GOD'S WORD, WE SHINE HIS LIGHT ON THE AREAS OF OUR LIVES THAT NEED TO BE TRANSFORMED.

BREAKING THE STRONGHOLD

Too many people in the body of Christ have been taken in by the spirit of religion, unknowingly falling into the snare of the enemy. They go to church every time the doors swing open, but they have never experienced real inner transformation. What is worse, they believe that because they have performed religious rituals for so long, they are indeed spiritual. Deception is insidious! Most people who are bound by a spirit of deception are unaware of it.

The blessing of the Word of God is that it has the power to break the strongholds of religion, barrenness, hypocrisy, and deception. God wants to show us a better way to live in the kingdom. We can live fruitful, abundant lives that prompt the world around us to want to know Jesus more each day!

VICTORY PRAYER

Heavenly Father, I thank You that, as a new creation, I am free from the religious spirit and its consequences. I am not just a hearer of the Word but also a doer of the Word. Rather than having merely a form of godliness, I have the explosive, supernatural power that accompanies true godliness, transforming me and those around me. Because I have been made new in Christ, I practice true religion—exercising self-control, reaching out to those in need, and keeping myself unspotted from the world. In Jesus's name, amen!

UNLOCKING THE CODE OF THE SUPERNATURAL INSIGHTS

1. What are the qualifications of someone who demonstrates *"pure religion,"* as described in James 1:26–27?

2. Describe the three characteristics of the spirit of religion as illustrated by the fig tree Jesus cursed.

3. What does it mean to have *"a form of godliness, but denying the power thereof"* (2 Timothy 3:5)?

4. What has the power to break the strongholds of religion, barrenness, hypocrisy, and deception in our lives?

MIRACLE TESTIMONY

BREAKING THE SHACKLES OF RELIGIOSITY

A dear sister in our church shared about how she used to live a sinful lifestyle full of witchcraft, rebellion, immorality, and hatred for God. She had grown up in Catholicism, and, due to her background in religion and church tradition, she'd never had a personal relationship with the Lord. And so, she found herself in that dark place.

Nevertheless, she desired to get closer to God at some point in her life. One day, she decided to go on a fast, during which she literally heard the voice of God prompting her to surrender her life to Christ. She prayed a prayer of salvation, and, several days later, she was baptized in the Holy Spirit at our church. Since then, this sister has ministered to many people, including her loved ones, who have come to salvation. She is bearing good fruit! It all began when she broke the shackles of the religious spirit and experienced a personal relationship with Jesus.

6

BREAKING THE CYCLE OF STRIVING

"O foolish Galatians, who has bewitched you,
that you should not obey the truth, before whose eyes Jesus Christ has
been evidently set forth, crucified among you?
This only would I learn of you, Received you the Spirit by the works
of the law, or by the hearing of faith? Are you so foolish?
having begun in the Spirit, are you now made perfect by the flesh?"
—Galatians 3:1–3

In the above passage, the apostle Paul was writing to the Galatian believers to address a very serious issue that had arisen among them. When they first believed in Christ, they had allowed the Holy Spirit to lead them, but now they had gone back to striving for their salvation. Certain people had told them that going through the motions of religion was necessary to please God. Scholars refer to these individuals as "Judaizers." They were a sect of Christians who came from the Jewish tradition. They had accepted Jesus, but they told non-Jewish converts to Christ that they needed to be circumcised in order to be saved.

The Judaizers were still living according to the law instead of grace, and they were trying to bring others under the law as well. (In the next chapter, we will further explore what happens when we try to live according to the law rather than by the Spirit.) As a result of this teaching, the Galatian church had been thrust into a vicious cycle of bondage. In addressing this problem, Paul poses a rhetorical question: *"Who has bewitched you?"*

It is noteworthy that he uses the term *"bewitched."* The word emphasizes the insidious nature of legalism. The Greek word translated *"bewitched"* is *baskaino*, among whose meanings is "to traduce" or "to charm." The Galatians were being taken in by the arguments and suggestions of this group of religious people and thereby manipulated into striving to be acceptable to God. They were being seduced into working for their salvation rather than flowing in the Spirit of Grace.

HAVE YOU BEEN MAKING ANY REQUIREMENTS FOR SALVATION—EITHER FOR YOURSELF OR OTHERS— THAT GO BEYOND THE GOSPEL OF JESUS CHRIST?

RELIGION WITHOUT RELATIONSHIP

Although the book of Galatians was written nearly two thousand years ago, many Christians today are in the same place of religious bondage that those early Christians were. As I explained previously, when this happens, people become trapped in a cycle of striving to please God. As a result, many well-intentioned believers are not able to obey God to the extent that they should. As we saw in chapter 5, the irony of religion is that the more religious we are, the less fruitful we are in our relationship with the Lord.

Religion without a relationship with God is like being in an emotionally abusive marital relationship in which a wife (the believer) is being manipulated by her husband (religion) but has been with him for so long that she cannot fully see the harmful effects on her soul. Religion can "bewitch" us if we are not careful.

Some of the Judaizers were putting standards and requirements on the Galatian church that they were not keeping themselves. In Galatians 2, Paul talks about having confronted Peter about this very issue:

> But when Peter was come to Antioch, I withstood him to the face, because he was to be blamed. For before that certain came from James, he did eat with the Gentiles: but when they were come, he withdrew and separated himself, fearing them which were of the circumcision. And the other Jews dissembled likewise with him; insomuch that Barnabas also was carried away with their dissimulation. But when I saw that they walked not uprightly according to the truth of the gospel, I said to Peter before them all, If you, being a Jew, live after the manner of Gentiles, and not as do the Jews, why compel you the Gentiles to live as do the Jews? —Galatians 2:11–14

Isn't it interesting that Peter, the great spiritual leader of his day, was also trapped in the clutches of religion? The situation was so perilous that Paul (a much lesser-regarded apostle at the time) publicly rebuked him. He reproved Peter because he was being pretentious in his dealings with the Jews. When he was alone with the Gentiles, he would eat the same things they ate and drink the same things they drank. However, when the

Jews came around, he separated himself from the company of the Gentiles because they had not been circumcised. He was looking the part but not being the part.

Again, while the Judaizers themselves were not keeping all the customs of the law, they were requiring the Gentiles to adopt various Jewish customs. Wouldn't it be funny if you found out that the religious people around you weren't even doing what they were telling you to do?

 THE IRONY OF RELIGION IS THAT THE MORE RELIGIOUS WE ARE, THE LESS FRUITFUL WE ARE IN OUR RELATIONSHIP WITH GOD.

WHAT DOES IT MEAN TO STRIVE?

A legalistic attitude leads to religious striving. Let's take a moment to consider what it means to strive. The word *strive* can be defined as "to make great efforts to achieve or obtain something" or "to struggle or fight vigorously." The problem with Christians striving is that the kingdom of God was never meant to be manifested through human effort. Paul admonishes the Galatians to obey what they had originally been taught, saying, *"O foolish Galatians, who has bewitched you, that you should not obey the truth, before whose eyes Jesus Christ has been evidently set forth, crucified among you?"* (Galatians 3:1). What truth is Paul referring to? That Christ has already accomplished the work for us!

God simply wanted the Galatian believers to respond to His grace, not to struggle for His acceptance. He wants us to do the same. Christ has already been crucified for us. He has already paid the price for our sins. Religious people often do not want you to know that the work has been accomplished for you. They may not even understand this truth for themselves. Like the Judaizers of old, many people assert that we must perform a series of rituals or exercises before God can accept us. As a result, a number of believers think that if they promise God that they will never sin again, or if they attend every service at their church, then God will find it in His religious heart to forgive them. But we have seen that God is not interested in religion at all. He wants so much more from us—and for us—than our vain attempts to impress Him.

As Paul declared in Galatians 3:3, *"Having begun in the Spirit, are you now made perfect by the flesh?"* The implication is that spiritual perfection can only come about through the Holy Spirit. The Spirit is the One who connects us to the Father's heart and brings us to a place of true intimacy with Him.

We must come to recognize, deep in our hearts, that no matter how hard we try, we will never be able to please God by our own efforts. In Romans 8:8, Paul wrote, *"So then they that are in the flesh cannot please God."* We can't become everything that God wants us to be through our *"flesh,"* that is, our fallen, carnal nature. This idea is hard for many people to understand because religion teaches us that our efforts are essential. Of course, our efforts in the Lord are important. We are called to do the works of God by His Spirit. *"For we are His workmanship, created in Christ Jesus to good works, which God has before ordained that we should walk in them"* (Ephesians 2:10). However, our works are misplaced when we consider them to be the means of our acceptance with God—and if they are not directed by the Spirit. If we want God's supernatural power to flow through us, we must understand the difference.

ARE YOU TRYING TO CONNECT WITH GOD THROUGH YOUR WORKS RATHER THAN BY HIS SPIRIT?

REMEDIES FOR STRIVING

STAND FAST IN LIBERTY

Stand fast therefore in the liberty wherewith Christ has made us free, and be not entangled again with the yoke of bondage.

—Galatians 5:1

I believe that what Paul emphatically proclaims here is a remedy for religious oppression. He tells the Galatian church to *"stand fast"* in the liberty Christ has supplied for them. I love that phrase! The Greek word translated *"stand fast"* is *steko*, among whose meanings is "to stand firm," "to persevere," and "to keep one's standing."

This command implies that our freedom in Christ is a finished work, a spiritual reality. The moment we accept Jesus Christ as our Lord and Savior by faith, we become free. Paul told the Galatians that they ought to stand firm in this truth. In other words, he encouraged them not to lose their spiritual standing by ceasing to live in the freedom of the Spirit. He knew there were demonic forces that desired to draw these believers away from the truth. Today, these same forces attempt to move us away from our standing in Christ.

ACCEPT THE LOVE OF GOD

Another remedy for religious oppression is to fully accept God's unconditional love for us. Striving manifests itself in a compulsive preoccupation with earning that love. Another way to describe this phenomenon is performance-orientation. In the field of the arts, one way of performing is to act in a play. There is nothing wrong with acting in a dramatic performance. However, in my opinion, "performing" profoundly describes the state of too many believers in the body of Christ. They are acting in a sort of spiritual stage play instead of living an authentic Christian life.

Earlier, we talked about how some people wear masks of hypocrisy in which they say one thing but do another. People can also wear masks to cover up the turmoil inside them. They put on the costume of "Christian," but behind their mask is an internal agony of guilt and insecurity. When we are not confident that we have been justified by faith and that God loves us, we believe that we must perform flawlessly for Him to accept us.

What is the problem with this way of thinking? First, it simply is not true! Second, every performance comes to an end. Actors may display phenomenal artistic ability in creating a dramatic character while a show is going on, but once the show is over, they retreat to their dressing rooms, remove their costumes and makeup, and become themselves again. The characters they portray are not their real selves.

This is similar to what is going on in the church. Christians are attempting to look the part of a "spiritual" person as they try to work their way into heaven. They think that if they volunteer at their church or give to the poor, it will absolve them of their sins and assuage their guilt-ridden consciences. People become involved in church committees, boards, and ministries, but they are not being spiritually transformed, and they experience troubles in their home lives. As a result, they become angry and frustrated. Although church involvement is wonderful and to be highly encouraged, in itself, it does not enhance our lives. We must first become new creations and learn what this means for us in practice. Then, and only then, will our lives be transformed.

God sees through our performances directly to our hearts. There is nothing we can do with our energy, time, and money to justify ourselves before God. We need to stop trying to earn our righteousness and receive His grace and forgiveness. We were not created to perform for God, but simply to love Him.

WE WERE NOT CREATED TO PERFORM FOR GOD, BUT SIMPLY TO LOVE HIM.

Are you sacrificing your inner peace on the altar of religious performance? What does God have to do to prove to you that He loves you? I submit that He has already done it! He sent His Son Jesus to die on the cross, be resurrected for us, and live victoriously within us through the Holy Spirit. I believe that people's striving in religious performance is behind so much of the sickness and disease that is prevalent in our churches. Christians are working so hard to *look* the part, rather than *be* the part, that it is taking a toll on their minds and bodies.

CONSIDER YOURSELF DEAD TO SIN

Performance will always be an inadequate means to cover our spiritual nakedness. Instead, we must realize we have been covered by the blood of Jesus. We are dead to the law, and as a result, we are dead to sin! We have been made righteous in God's sight, and we do works of righteousness on the basis of our relationship with Him. Love for God is what should prompt the believer's obedience. We keep His commandments because we love Him through Jesus Christ, not because we are trying to prove to Him that we are good people.

If you will come to terms with this simple truth, it will radically reshape your life. I have seen more victory in my life by understanding this truth than by almost any other means. God loves you! You are no longer under the law of dos and don'ts. You have been completely delivered from that system of living. You are fully under the grace of God, empowered to carry out His will on a daily basis. You have been wedded permanently to Jesus Christ, and your only assignment is to please your new Spouse.

WALK IN THE SPIRIT

The Galatians found themselves concentrating on external issues while neglecting the life of the Spirit. As a result, they were no longer focused on living victoriously from within. By accepting a deception, they had departed from God's truth. Paul gave them only one solution: *"If you be led of the Spirit, you are not under the law"* (Galatians 5:18). When we walk in the Spirit, we cease striving.

Remember that Paul had previously asked the Galatian church, *"Having begun in the Spirit, are you now made perfect by the flesh?"* In the context of this verse, the flesh represents justification by works, and the Spirit represents justification by faith. Again, Paul is challenging the notion that a Christian is able to accomplish anything through human efforts. The more we realize there is nothing we can do through our own abilities to justify ourselves, the more we can rest in the reality of the finished work of Christ!

What does it mean to walk in the Spirit? It means to stand fast in our secure position in Christ and to live according to the love and grace of God. It means to rest in God's supernatural ability and not our own. The more we rely on the Holy Spirit, the more the fruit and gifts of the Spirit will be manifested in us and through us. This seems like such a simple solution, doesn't it? The problem does not lie in the simplicity of the solution. The problem lies in our truly believing that it is sufficient. There is no greater way to live a life of victory than to walk according to the Spirit of God.

VICTORY PRAYER

Father, in the name of Jesus Christ, I declare that I will no longer be bound by a vicious cycle of striving to obtain Your love and acceptance. I stand fast in the liberty with which Christ has made me free. I rest in the finished work of Jesus. Your truth is the only truth that matters in my life. I reject the lie that tells me Your grace is somehow insufficient for me. Thank You for my freedom, wholeness, and victory in Christ. In Jesus's name, amen!

UNLOCKING THE CODE OF THE SUPERNATURAL INSIGHTS

1. What happens in our relationship with God the more religious we are?

2. In Galatians 2, for what reason did Paul need to rebuke Peter?

3. How do we attain spiritual perfection?

4. What does it mean to walk in the Spirit?

7

FREEDOM FROM THE LAW

*"Know you not, brethren, (for I speak to them that know the law,)
how that the law has dominion over a man as long as he lives? For the
woman which has a husband is bound by the law to her husband so
long as he lives; but if the husband be dead, she is loosed from the law
of her husband. So then if, while her husband lives, she be married
to another man, she shall be called an adulteress: but if her husband
be dead, she is free from that law; so that she is no adulteress, though
she be married to another man. Wherefore, my brethren, you also
are become dead to the law by the body of Christ; that you should be
married to another, even to Him who is raised from the dead, that
we should bring forth fruit to God. For when we were in the flesh, the
motions of sins, which were by the law, did work in our members to
bring forth fruit to death. But now we are delivered from the law, that
being dead wherein we were held; that we should serve in newness of
spirit, and not in the oldness of the letter."*
—Romans 7:1–6

The book of Romans is one of the most important and profound books
of the Bible. In this epistle, Paul explains the gospel of grace. In order to

understand this spiritual truth, we must see the stark contrast between law and grace. Paul provides a powerful analogy involving marriage and death to highlight this reality. Under the Mosaic law, a woman was bound to her husband as long as he lived. She was not allowed to step outside the confines of her marriage to have a relationship with any another man, or she would be guilty of adultery. Under the old covenant, if a woman committed adultery, she was to be stoned to death. This was the judgment associated with the law. However, if her husband died, she was free to marry another man.

BOUND TO THE LAW

Paul uses this illustration to show us that, before Christ came, we were bound, or married, to the law. Because of our sinful nature, we were already imprisoned by sin-consciousness and a compulsive propensity to violate God's commandments. The law amplified this situation by bringing us under condemnation every time we violated it. But the Bible says that we are *"dead to the law by the body of Christ"* (Romans 7:4). What does this mean? It means that because, spiritually speaking, we were crucified with Jesus on the cross, we have been freed from the law. The moment we gave our lives to Jesus, we entered into this reality. Our death in Christ gave us the legal right to be married to Him. *"We are buried with Him by baptism into death: that like as Christ was raised up from the dead by the glory of the Father, even so we also should walk in newness of life"* (Romans 6:4). We are no longer under the control, government, and dictates of the law; we are now under the control of Jesus. He is our Husband in a spiritual sense (this is gender neutral).

Paul says that when we were under the law, we brought forth *"fruit to death"* (Romans 7:5). In other words, when we were in the flesh, married to the law, we were impregnated with sin, guilt, shame, and condemnation, which ultimately produced death. That was the fruit of our union with the law. Yet, when we gave our lives to Jesus Christ, we came together in spiritual union with Him, resulting in our being impregnated with the very life and peace of God.

The church desperately needs to understand this truth. I believe that many believers are guilty of spiritual adultery because they are trying to simultaneously be married to the law and to Christ. This is why they attempt (and fail) to both perform for God and operate under His grace. Again, such an attempt is a recipe for frustration and spiritual barrenness. God makes it clear in His Word that, through Christ, we are truly dead to the law. We can tell when we are trying to come back under the law because of the type of fruit we bear. In Romans 7:6, we see the evidence of being under the grace of God rather than under the law. Paul says that when we are freed from the law, we are empowered to *"serve [God] in newness of spirit."*

NEWNESS OF SPIRIT

The Greek word translated *"newness"* in Romans 7:6 is *kainotes*, which indicates "in the new state of life in which the Holy Spirit places us so as to produce a new state which is eternal life." Wow! When we are joined to Jesus Christ as our Lord and Savior, we are ushered into a new realm of living. Our union with Him releases eternal life! This means that we can live a life that transcends the circumstances and situations around us. It is a life that is victorious in every area. When we live in this way, it is evidence that we are walking in the Spirit.

IN WHAT WAYS MIGHT YOU BE TRYING TO LIVE ACCORDING TO LAW AND GRACE AT THE SAME TIME?

As we have seen, the evidence that we are still married to the law is *"fruit to death"* (verse 5). Additional evidence is *"the oldness of the letter"* (verse 6). The Greek word for *"oldness"* is *palaiotes*, which refers to "the old state of life controlled by 'the letter.'" The word for *"letter"* is *gramma*, which can mean "a…bill, bond, account, written acknowledgement of a debt." Thus, the oldness of the letter is a state of living in which we are governed or bound by an acknowledgement of our debt. We are constantly living in a state of indebtedness. The problem with the debt of the law is that no amount of righteous deeds on our part can repay the debt we owe. The human race entered into spiritual debt the moment Adam sinned against God. We inherited the debt of sin and death from our great-great-great (many times over) grandfather.

WHEN WE ARE JOINED TO JESUS CHRIST AS OUR LORD AND SAVIOR, WE ARE USHERED INTO A NEW REALM OF LIVING. WE CAN LIVE A LIFE THAT TRANSCENDS THE CIRCUMSTANCES AND SITUATIONS AROUND US.

Romans 3:20 says, *"Therefore by the deeds of the law there shall no flesh be justified in [God's] sight: for by the law is the knowledge of sin."* Why can no one ever be justified by the law? Because the law is perfect and we are imperfect. Each one of us is guilty under the law. In fact, the reason God gave the law to the Israelites in the wilderness was to show them they could not be righteous in themselves.

Romans 7:13 says, *"Was then that which is good [the law] made death to me? God forbid. But sin, that it might appear sin, working death in me by that which is good; that sin by the commandment might become exceeding sinful."* The purpose of the law was to make our sin *"exceeding sinful."* In other words, the law is a magnifying glass that reveals to us our unrighteousness apart from God.

"What shall we say then? Is the law sin? God forbid. Nay, I had not known sin, but by the law: for I had not known lust, except the law had said, You shall not covet" (Romans 7:7). Paul is saying that when he heard the

commandment *"You shall not covet,"* it awakened in him a desire to obtain the very thing he was not allowed to have. We have the same experience with the law. Due to our fallen nature, we harbor sinful desires, but the law draws them out of us and exposes them. We are tempted to do the opposite of what the law says. As a parent, I frequently see this effect. Sometimes, when I tell my children not to touch something, it creates a greater urge in them to touch it. Again, this is what the law does. It arouses sinful desires inside us.

The law also produces in us *"the knowledge of sin"* (Romans 3:20). The Greek word rendered *"knowledge"* is *epignosis*, which, in the New Testament, refers to "the knowledge of things ethical and divine." After Adam and Eve violated God's commandment, they immediately felt condemned because they had an increased awareness of their sin. God's perfect will for them was to be conscious of His presence alone, but Satan knew that once they were exposed to the knowledge of sin, they would immediately be alienated from the life of God. Does that experience sound familiar to you?

HOW DO YOU FEEL AFTER YOU HAVE SINNED?

WHAT IS THE FIRST THING YOU DO?

NO CONDEMNATION!

There is therefore now no condemnation to them which are in Christ Jesus, who walk not after the flesh, but after the Spirit.
—Romans 8:1

According to the *Merriam-Webster* online dictionary, the verb *condemn* means "to declare to be reprehensible, wrong, or evil usually after weighing evidence and without reservation." The Greek word translated *"condemnation"* in Romans 8:1 is *katakrima*, which signifies a "damnatory sentence." When we continue to feel condemned by our sin, even after we have repented of it, it prevents us from moving on in our lives. It keeps us stuck in a state of spiritual, emotional, and even physical stagnation, believing we are unable to be a vessel that God can use to set other people free. Simply put, a sense of condemnation is an overwhelming feeling of unworthiness that prohibits us from receiving God's love and mercy. And this is a primary symptom of living under the law.

As long as we carry a belief about ourselves that does not agree with the Word of God, Satan has the ability to manipulate and control us. The truth is that there is *no condemnation* to those who are in Christ Jesus. We are no longer to be governed by our emotions or the world system but by the Word of God and the Holy Spirit. Jesus paid a tremendous price to enable us to walk with God in perfect fellowship and harmony. Satan wants the body of Christ to be ignorant of this truth.

A SENSE OF CONDEMNATION IS AN OVERWHELMING FEELING OF UNWORTHINESS THAT PROHIBITS US FROM RECEIVING GOD'S LOVE AND MERCY. THIS IS A PRIMARY SYMPTOM OF LIVING UNDER THE LAW.

Thus, when we accept a sense of condemnation, we give power to the enemy in our lives. Satan's goal is to bring you under condemnation through temptation and sin. He knows that in an atmosphere of condemnation, believers will be rendered ineffective. This is the reason there are many ineffective Christians in the church. They are so preoccupied with the shame of their sin that they are distracted from fulfilling God's purpose in their lives. For example, many Christians know they should invite others to church and/or tell them about Jesus, but they do not do so. Why is this the case? I believe that, to a great extent, it is because of feelings of condemnation. These believers feel disqualified from the ranks of those who share their faith in Jesus. They feel like they have enough problems to deal with, so they don't bother to reach beyond their own lives into the lives of those around them. This is not the will of God. We ought to count it a privilege to share our excitement about the Lord, but if we feel condemned by Satan, we will never do this.

Adam and Eve could definitely identify with this scenario. Genesis 3:8 says, *"And they heard the voice of the* Lord *God walking in the garden in the cool of the day: and Adam and his wife hid themselves from the presence of the* Lord *God among the trees of the garden."* After they sinned, Adam and Eve ran *from* God's presence rather than *to* His presence. Many Christians are doing the same thing, running away from the Lord rather than running toward Him. After they sin, they stop attending church regularly or they find another community of Christians where they don't have to come out into the open and be accountable to other believers but can sit on the sidelines. All the while, Satan is accusing them before God and telling them that they are not fit to be used by Him. They have bought into the lie that they can no longer be restored, thinking of themselves as an old, discarded dishcloth. Rather than receive the grace God has made available to them through repentance and forgiveness, they choose to hide in the cavern of condemnation.

If this is your situation, come out of your hiding place, in Jesus's name! God's plan for you is so much greater than your failure or your sin. He is able to cleanse you completely if you will sincerely repent. Condemnation is rooted in fear and deception. Every area of bondage in our lives is empowered by a lie that we have believed. What is that lie? It is that God has pronounced a death sentence over us. Beloved, Jesus Christ took our death sentence on Himself so that we could live abundantly. Jesus's blood is fully sufficient to cover your sin and shame. When you understand this truth, you will approach God confidently as your Father and Deliverer.

GOD'S PLAN FOR YOU IS SO MUCH GREATER THAN YOUR FAILURE OR YOUR SIN.

VICTORY PRAYER

Father, in the name of Your Son Jesus Christ, I declare that I am free from the law. I live under the abundant flow of Your grace, which empowers me to live righteously. I take authority over Satan and all of his wicked devices in the form of guilt, shame, and condemnation. I loose myself from the bondage of condemnation right now, and I declare that the person whom the Son sets free is free indeed. I will no longer strive for Your love and acceptance, but I will receive the fullness of Your redemption in every area of my life. In the precious name of Jesus Christ, amen!

UNLOCKING THE CODE OF THE SUPERNATURAL INSIGHTS

1. What does it mean to be married to the law? What does it mean to be married to Christ?

2. In Romans 7:6, what does *kainotes*, the Greek word translated *"newness,"* signify?

3. What evidence shows that we are still living as if we are married to the law?

4. What lie from Satan keeps many believers under a sense of condemnation? What is the answer to this lie?

8

PUTTING ON CHRIST AS OUR RIGHTEOUSNESS

"Brethren, my heart's desire and prayer to God for Israel is, that they might be saved. For I bear them record that they have a zeal of God, but not according to knowledge. For they being ignorant of God's righteousness, and going about to establish their own righteousness, have not submitted themselves to the righteousness of God. For Christ is the end of the law for righteousness to every one that believes."
—Romans 10:1–4

Those who are still trying to establish their own righteousness hinder their freedom in the Spirit and their ability to walk in the supernatural. As I previously mentioned, most of my young life was characterized by religion and my association with religious people. Even though I attended a Spirit-filled church, the stronghold of the law was so powerful there that many of the members, including me, were unable to progress in their walks with God.

I want to clarify that I had good intentions, as do many believers who are caught in the trap of religion. I thought I was doing absolutely the right thing in my efforts to please God. But then I discovered Romans 10! When

I really took hold of the truths in this chapter, it transformed my entire outlook.

ACCEPTABLE TO GOD

The context of chapters 8, 9, and 10 of the book of Romans is God's covenant with the Jewish people. In Romans 9, Paul says that he has a tremendous burden and concern for the people of Israel. His earnest prayer to God is that they would be saved. In Romans 10, he goes on to express, *"I bear them record that they have a zeal of God, but not according to knowledge"* (verse 2). The Greek word rendered *"knowledge"* is *epignosis*, the same word we looked at earlier in the phrase *"the knowledge of sin"* (Romans 3:20). As we noted, the New Testament meaning of this word is "the knowledge of things ethical and divine." In general terms, the word means "precise and correct knowledge." Paul is saying that in performing their religious practices, the Israelites were not acting out of a proper understanding of what God wanted. We have all fallen into this error at one point or another. He continues, *"They being ignorant of God's righteousness, and going about to establish their own righteousness, have not submitted themselves to the righteousness of God"* (Romans 10:3). This statement is pretty intense! They were ignorant of God's righteousness.

HOW WOULD YOU DEFINE *RIGHTEOUSNESS*?

WHAT IS THE BASIS OF A CHRISTIAN'S RIGHTEOUSNESS?

The word *righteous* generally means to be in right standing or right positioning with God. The Greek word for *"righteousness"* in Romans 10:3, *dikaiosune*, means, "in a broad sense: state of him who is as he ought to be, righteousness, the condition acceptable to God." Based on this definition, the Israelites had a twofold problem. First, they were ignorant of their true position in God. As a result, they tried to establish their own secure position based on works. Second, they were ignorant of the way they ought to be. Because they were trying to become righteous on the basis of their own efforts, they completely missed the revelation of God's provision of righteousness in Christ. They did not realize that being righteous wasn't a matter of doing external works but rather of spiritual positioning.

Many of us, in practice, have fallen out of this spiritual position. When we are out of position, we do what only comes natural—we strive.

THE SEAT OF RIGHTEOUSNESS

Some time ago, I was invited to a free pastors' luncheon. All I had to do was reserve my seat in advance. When I arrived at the event, I merely needed to show the staff my reservation, and they escorted me to my reserved table. This is a perfect analogy for our spiritual position in Christ. God has already reserved a place in which we will receive all that He wants to give us, including grace, forgiveness, salvation, eternal life, and blessings. This position or seat is called "righteousness." If we reject our reservation and try to find our own seat, attempting to establish our own righteousness, we will be in the wrong place for receiving from God.

Righteousness is a position. It is a seat of acceptance, favor, and blessing in our relationship with the Lord. We must keep in mind that He has already prepared this place for us. We just need to make our reservation—and then be willing to sit down in the seat of favor, love, and authority God has provided for us! We do this by submitting to His righteousness, not our own. Romans 10:4 says, *"For **Christ is the end of the law for righteousness** to every one that believes."*

Christ is the *end* of the law—of striving—to everyone who believes! To enter into our position of righteousness and all that comes with it, we simply need to believe in Jesus Christ. Like the pastors' luncheon I attended where my meal was already paid for, Christ has already paid the price to make His righteousness available to us. Again, our role is to receive it.

RIGHTEOUSNESS IS A POSITION. IT IS A SEAT OF ACCEPTANCE, FAVOR, AND BLESSING IN OUR RELATIONSHIP WITH THE LORD.

This idea is hard for many of us to comprehend and accept because we just can't imagine a state of affairs in which we are not rewarded based on human effort. From the time we were born, we were indoctrinated into the merit system. We were taught to compete for social, academic, and financial rewards. Some of us even grew up in homes where siblings were encouraged to compete with one another for love, acceptance, and recognition. As a result, we bring the same frame of mind into our relationship with God. We say, "Surely, I have to do *something* to earn my salvation!" Yet our righteousness will never be good enough. It will never bring us salvation. The kingdom of God operates under a completely different paradigm. Remember that the Bible refers to human righteousness as *"filthy rags"* (Isaiah 64:6). And Romans 3:10 says, *"There is none righteous, no, not one."*

In and of ourselves, we are unable to live up to God's righteous standard. In our frail human flesh, we do not have the capacity to offer a worthy sacrifice to atone for our sins. While your obedience and faithfulness toward God are rewarded by Him, they do not save you. They were not meant to! A tremendous price was paid to reserve your seat of righteousness, and that price was the precious blood of the Lamb. If it is hard for you to digest the notion of receiving something for free, let me assure you— your righteousness has been paid for in full! God wants you to exchange your righteousness for Christ's righteousness.

RIGHTEOUSNESS BY FAITH

For I am not ashamed of the gospel of Christ: for it is the power of God to salvation to every one that believes; to the Jew first, and also to the

> Greek. *For therein is the righteousness of God revealed from faith to faith: as it is written, The just shall live by faith.* —Romans 1:16–17

This imparted righteousness is what the message of Christ is all about and the reason why Paul says that he is not ashamed of the gospel. We should not be ashamed of it either! Why? Because it is the power of God that brings about our salvation. Salvation comes when people put their faith in Christ as they hear the Word of God. (See Romans 10:17.) Notice that Paul does not say the gospel is *a* power of God for salvation, but *the* power of God for salvation.

This is why it is imperative for ministers to preach the unadulterated gospel. Motivational speaking will not save us. Social programs will not save us. Government policies will not save us. These elements bring some good to people, but they cannot give them eternal salvation and the indwelling Holy Spirit to live a supernatural life. Only the gospel of Jesus Christ has the power to do this.

Why is the gospel so powerful? Paul tells us in Romans 1:17: *"For therein is the righteousness of God revealed from faith to faith: as it is written, The just shall live by faith."* The righteousness of God is the answer to the perils that plague our world and our church.

Paul had a revelation of God's righteousness that changed his life. When we receive this revelation, it changes our lives as well. This righteousness is revealed *"from faith to faith."* It is our faith in Christ that imparts His righteousness to us. You might be surprised how many people are ignorant of this truth. We must thoroughly understand that Christ gives us His righteousness the moment we place our faith in Him. We stand innocent in God's presence solely on the basis of Jesus's blood, which has washed us and made us clean, and His righteousness, which has been imparted to us. Second Corinthians 5:21 puts it this way:

> *For He has made Him to be sin for us, who knew no sin; that we might be made the righteousness of God in Him.*

Christ was sinless, yet He was *"made...to be sin"* on our behalf. This means that He had to become something that was contrary to His very nature. The Bible says that He *"knew not sin."* It wasn't something He was familiar with. On our behalf, Christ took on a nature that was abhorrent to Him. When He was crucified on the cross, the sin of the entire world lay on His shoulders. What a weight He bore for us!

He took on all of that so that we could become righteous. Actually, let me put it in biblical terminology: we were *"made"* righteous! We do not gradually progress into a righteous state so that, after a period of time, we eventually become righteous if we keep doing the right things. This is not scriptural; it is just another form of religion. Many people think this way without even realizing it. They believe that if they do enough "penance," they will finally earn enough spiritual points to offset their sins.

IN WHAT WAYS MIGHT YOU BE TRYING TO DO "PENANCE"
FOR YOUR SINS AND MISTAKES RATHER THAN RECEIVING
GOD'S FORGIVENESS FOR THEM AND ACCEPTING YOUR
RIGHTEOUSNESS IN CHRIST?

In 2 Corinthians 5:21, the word *"made"* in the phrase *"made the righteousness of God in Him"* is translated from the Greek term *ginomai*, a word we've noted in previous chapters from two different passages in the book of John. We have seen that this term signifies "to come into existence." Another of its meanings is "to be finished." The moment we gave ourselves to Jesus Christ, God supernaturally caused us to be just like Him in nature and spiritual identity. This identity was finished and settled from that time on. We stepped into the complete perfection of Jesus in relation to our position in the eyes of the Father.

PUT ON JESUS!

In Genesis 27, there is an account of a momentous event in the lives of Jacob and Esau. For many years, I read this account only in a straightforward way, taking in the facts of the story. There is nothing wrong with such a reading, but I missed its additional spiritual significance. This passage is loaded with supernatural revelation of the new covenant!

And it came to pass, that when Isaac was old, and his eyes were dim, so that he could not see, he called Esau his eldest son, and said to him, My son: and he said to him, Behold, here am I. And he said, Behold now, I am old, I know not the day of my death: now therefore take, I pray you, your weapons, your quiver and your bow, and go out to the field, and take me some venison; and make me savory meat, such as I love, and bring it to me, that I may eat; that my soul may bless you before I die. And Rebekah heard when Isaac spoke to Esau his son. And Esau went to the field to hunt for venison, and to bring it. And Rebekah spoke to Jacob her son, saying, Behold, I heard your father speak to Esau your brother, saying, Bring me venison, and make me savory meat, that I may eat, and bless you before the LORD before my death. Now therefore, my son, obey my voice according to that which I command you. Go now to the flock, and bring me from there two good kids of the goats; and I will make them savory meat for your father, such as he loves: and you shall bring it to your father, that he may eat, and that he may bless you before his death. And Jacob said to Rebekah his mother, Behold, Esau my brother is a hairy man, and I am a smooth man: my father perhaps will feel me, and I shall seem to him as a deceiver; and I shall bring a curse upon me, and not a blessing. And his mother said to him, Upon me be your curse, my son: only obey my voice, and go bring me them. And he went, and brought, and brought them to his mother: and his mother made savory meat, such as his father loved. And Rebekah took goodly raiment of her eldest son Esau, which were with her in the house, and put them upon Jacob her younger son: and she put the skins of the kids of the goats upon his hands, and upon the smooth of his neck: and she gave the savory meat and the bread, which she had prepared, into the hand of her son Jacob. And he came to his father, and said, My father: and he said, Here am I; who are you, my son? And Jacob said to his father, I am Esau your firstborn; I have done according as you bid me: arise, I pray you, sit and eat of my venison, that your soul may bless me. —Genesis 27:1–19

In this passage, Esau, who is Isaac's firstborn, is about to be blessed by his father. In ancient Hebrew culture, the father would convey to his eldest son both the family birthright and a special blessing. The birthright involved not only an inheritance of the best and greatest portion of the father's materials goods, but also a spiritual impartation. The verbal blessing was a decree of success, vision, and prosperity. Receiving this blessing was one of the most important times in an eldest son's life. When we understand the significance of the blessing, it puts this story into perspective for us.

Jacob had already managed to obtain Esau's birthright from him. (See Genesis 25:29–34.) But in this passage, he also manipulated Isaac into giving the verbal blessing to him rather than his older brother, which is why Esau was so angry after this event. Isaac was about to die, and he had sent Esau to hunt for meat and prepare a final meal for him. Once Isaac's wife, Rebekah, heard about this plan, she immediately coerced her younger son into impersonating his brother. Why? Jacob was her favorite, and she wanted him to have the blessing of the firstborn!

This deception would not be easy because Jacob and Esau were two totally different people with distinct physical appearances and demeanors. Due to his old age, Isaac's eyesight was dim. Rebekah capitalized on his condition by having Jacob put on Esau's best clothing as a disguise. In fact, she went even further by putting goatskins on Jacob's arms and neck to complete the pretense because Esau's skin was especially hairy. We see the outcome of this impersonation in verses 21 through 23:

And Isaac said to Jacob, Come near, I pray you, that I may feel you, my son, whether you be my very son Esau or not. And Jacob went near to Isaac his father; and he felt him, and said, The voice is Jacob's voice, but the hands are the hands of Esau. And he discerned him not, because his hands were hairy, as his brother Esau's hands: so he blessed him.

The content of this blessing is found in verses 28 and 29. Why did Jacob receive the blessing? Because he "put on" his elder brother. Although Jacob obtained the blessing through deceitful means, I believe there is great symbolism in this account regarding what took place when we gave our lives to Jesus Christ. We put on Jesus's best garments—His righteousness. As I expressed in other terms earlier, all that the heavenly Father can see, feel, smell, and perceive about our lives is Jesus, our Elder Brother!

Because of Christ's sacrifice for us on the cross, we experience a spiritual transference of His righteousness to us. In Romans 13:14, we are commanded, *"But put you on the Lord Jesus Christ, and make not provision for the flesh, to fulfil the lusts thereof."* The Greek word for *"put you on"* is *endyo*, which literally means "to sink into (clothing), put on, clothe one's self." If Jacob had worn his own clothing, instead of Esau's garments, when he went in to see Isaac, he would not have received the blessing. Likewise, our clothing of human works is not sufficient to position us to be eternally blessed by God. By faith, we are to clothe ourselves with Jesus Christ. We are to "sink into" His righteousness, not our own.

Isaac favored Esau, and Esau, as the firstborn, was the rightful recipient of the blessing. But when Isaac thought Jacob was actually Esau, he released the blessing to him without reservation. We are in a similar situation. God still loved us when we were spiritually dead in our sins. However, we were not in a right relationship with Him until we received what Christ did for us—paying the penalty for our sin and sharing His birthright with us. Not only did Christ's robe of righteousness become our robe of righteousness, but through His shed blood, which has been applied to us, we have been justified from all forms of condemnation. In other words, we have "full coverage"! In Christ, we have been given access to the complete inheritance that belongs to Him. *"And if children, then heirs; heirs of God, and joint-heirs with Christ; if so be that we suffer with Him, that we may be also glorified together"* (Romans 8:17).

BY FAITH, WE ARE TO CLOTHE OURSELVES WITH JESUS CHRIST. WE ARE TO "SINK INTO" HIS RIGHTEOUSNESS AND NOT OUR OWN.

Jesus Christ is our Elder Brother in redemption. I want you to really consider the magnitude of this truth! All that the Father has was given to Jesus Christ, and all that Jesus Christ has was given to us. We are joint-heirs with Jesus! A joint-heir has a legal right to share in the inheritance. We have been given unlimited access to God's blessing, not based on our own goodness, but on what Christ has accomplished for us.

Just as Isaac called Jacob to *"come near,"* we have been called by God to draw near to Him. God wants us to have intimate fellowship with Him on the basis of Christ's righteousness. Like Jacob, we were sinful, manipulative, selfish, and fearful. Yet, now that we are in Jesus, we *"who once were far off have been brought near by the blood of Christ"* (Ephesians 2:13 NKJV).

Oh, what victory you will experience when you possess this revelation! We in the body of Christ are in desperate need of understanding Christ's righteousness and how it is applied to us. How can sin, shame, and condemnation control us when we are walking in the character, nature, and authority of Jesus, our Elder Brother? How can sickness and disease exert power over us once we realize that we are "wearing" the life of the Lord Jesus Christ?

ALL THAT THE FATHER HAS WAS GIVEN TO JESUS CHRIST, AND ALL THAT JESUS CHRIST HAS WAS GIVEN TO US.

UNLOCKING THE CODE OF THE SUPERNATURAL INSIGHTS

1. What is the biblical definition of *righteousness?*

2. Why is the gospel so powerful, as Paul writes about in Romans 1:16–17?

3. What is the difference between the idea of "becoming" righteous and being "made" righteous?

4. What inheritance have we been given in Christ?

PART II:
LIVING A SUPERNATURAL LIFESTYLE

9

CREATION VERSUS REFORMATION

"And have put on the new man, which is renewed in knowledge after the image of Him that created him."
—Colossians 3:10

After the death of the original apostles—those who were eyewitnesses to Jesus's resurrection—the church took on a shape that was much different from what it was when they were alive. At the beginning of the fourth century, the Roman emperor Constantine converted to Christianity and removed many of the restrictions on Christians. His actions led to Christianity becoming the state religion of Rome in the year 380.

After the third century, the church was dominated by Catholicism for over one thousand years. With these cultural changes and the closing of many pagan temples, a number of people in the Roman Empire became Christians either out of genuine conversion or expediency.[2] Over the course of time, pagan worshippers were forced into the Catholic system of worship and practice. As you can imagine, there was much mingling of practice and

2. Henry Chadwick and The Editors of *Encyclopaedia Britannica*, "The Alliance Between Church and Empire," Britannica, https://www.britannica.com/topic/Christianity/The-alliance-between-church-and-empire.

doctrine between Roman and Babylonian idolatry and Catholicism. It was common for people to engage in the worship of saints and the purchase of relics and indulgences. Although the Bible had been translated into Latin, not many people could read it, and the pope had the authority to establish absolute doctrine for the church. Parishioners had to go to the priest to confess their sins in order to be forgiven by God. Often, people had to perform a number of penances in order to be exonerated. Loved ones could be "purchased" out of purgatory, and people could receive admission into so-called paradise by fighting wars on behalf of the papacy. Most of all, people were encouraged to seek salvation by works of righteousness instead of by grace.

Up to this time, the church and its leadership were fully under the government of the Roman Catholic system. Then, in the early fifteenth century, part of the church began to undergo a radical change in theology and ecclesiastical structure when an Augustinian monk by the name of Martin Luther, who knew Latin and Greek and could read the Bible, realized that these practices were not scriptural. He recognized that there was a deep need for reformation. The influence of Luther and others started a movement called the Reformation, which led to the development of Protestantism, the Reformed Church, and the publication of the King James Version of the Bible in 1611. The Catholic Church itself underwent a Counter-Reformation as a result of the upheaval.

JESUS DID NOT COME TO REFORM HUMANITY BUT TO RECREATE PEOPLE INTO HIS VERY IMAGE!

The word *reformation* is defined as "the action or process of reforming an institution or practice." Ultimately, that is what took place in the Protestant Reformation and Counter-Reformation. Practices changed, institutions were shifted, and new organizations were established. This shift was necessary to address religious errors and abuses in the church. However, there were some negative aspects to this series of events. I believe one of the foremost was that it created an emphasis on *reformation* rather than *recreation*. The church was never meant to be reformed organizationally; it was meant to be transformed spiritually. Jesus did not come to reform humanity but to recreate people into His very image!

YOU ARE A NEW CITY

Like the sixteenth-century church, many churches today have focused their time, money, and energy on reforming people externally rather than helping them understand what it means to be a new creation. Consequently, whole sectors of Christianity have developed a culture of performance—an issue we looked at closely in part I of this book. Just as some prisoners who are released back into society return to their old way of life, so those who simply experience reformation will inevitably go back to their old mindset and habits. As we have seen, instead of merely undergoing certain reforms, Christians are to experience a radical, supernatural transformation of spirit, soul, and body. Such a transformation is exactly what the global church needs! We must live according to our recreation in God's image, experiencing such a radical internal shift that we will not be able to retreat back into our old life.

HOW WOULD YOU LIKE TO BE FILLED WITH GOD'S SPIRIT

IN SUCH A POWERFUL WAY THAT YOU AND OTHER

BELIEVERS LITERALLY ALTER THE FABRIC OF

THE CULTURE IN WHICH YOU LIVE?

I am very thankful for many of the fathers of the Reformation because, without their obedience to the Holy Spirit, only God knows where the church would be today. Yet I believe another mega-shift is coming to the body of Christ. It will not be a reformation but the needed *recreation* we have been discussing. *"For in Christ Jesus neither circumcision avails any thing, nor uncircumcision, but a new creature"* (Galatians 6:15). God is bringing about change on a subatomic level, spiritually speaking. As were the believers in the early church, we can be filled with God's Spirit in such a powerful way that we literally alter the fabric of the culture in which we live. The early believers *"turned the world upside down"* (Acts 17:6). This shaking of the world wherever Christians walked was never supposed to end. We are meant to be ablaze with the fire of the Holy Spirit until Jesus returns. While most of us have simply tried to repaint our exteriors, God wants us to experience abundant life within!

Cultural Christianity will not save anyone. We need to become totally new spiritual entities. Colossians 3:10 says, *"And have put on the new man, which is renewed in knowledge after the image of Him that created him."* Christ came so that we could become renewed in our knowledge of the One who created us.

The Greek word rendered *"created"* in this verse is *ktizo.* One of its meanings in Greek society was "to found a city, colony, state." Isn't this an amazing way to see things? When God recreates you, He is the Founder of the city called "A New You." When someone is the founder of a city, they have the right to name the city, establish a government there, and build an infrastructure. Thus, not only are you the temple of the Holy Spirit, but you are also a city of God where His government, or rule, has been established! Before Jesus could live in your spirit, the Holy Spirit had to make it a suitable dwelling place by recreating your spirit-man by the same power that raised Jesus from the dead. You have been given so much more than you realize. Reformation is great, but recreation is greater!

 WHEN GOD RECREATES YOU, HE IS THE FOUNDER OF THE CITY CALLED "A NEW YOU."

NOT CHURCH-AS-USUAL

Today, there are many problems in the church. Nevertheless, again, God is not calling us to change our ecclesiastical institutions, structures, and practices. He is calling us to undergo spiritual transformation. As a pastor, I have struggled in my heart to understand why people I have ministered to don't seem to experience an ounce of change in their lives. As I will talk about more in a coming chapter, much of this may be attributed to a false idea of conviction. However, I believe another issue is that people are merely trying to "reform" their behavior. This is why you will hear individuals say things like, "I have to get my life together!" Doing this is an impossible task apart from God.

God wants to do away with the old and give birth to the new. Many people are trapped in what I call "church-as-usual" because they have not experienced authentic regeneration—or they are unaware of this spiritual change within them. God does not desire church-as-usual. He does not want us to just keep going through the motions. He wants victory in our lives! He wants us to be His ambassadors and ministers of the new covenant.

REFORMATION IS GREAT, BUT RECREATION IS GREATER!

Unfortunately, the way we have been conducting our churches does not lend itself to our moving into this reality. In many ways, we function like the Catholic church did in the sixteenth century. In general, we still have a hierarchal system that does not encourage people to read the Word of God for themselves. We still emphasize church positions and titles more than we do personal devotion, which is the source of real spiritual power and authority. We have created a spiritual codependence that keeps people from maturing in the ways of God and ultimately fulfilling their God-ordained assignments. The church may have been reformed, but it has not been fully recreated. We have to change!

This change will only come about when we see things from God's vantage point. I decided long ago that I wanted more out of Christianity than smoke and mirrors. I wanted to experience everything God has shown us is possible in the pages of the Bible. I remember being in the early stages of my faith and reading about the exciting exploits of the apostles in the book of Acts. As I read, I was overwhelmed with joy and excitement as I imagined doing the same things they were doing through the power of the Holy Spirit—that is, until I interacted with other Christians in my youth group. I discovered that they did not possess the same enthusiasm for God's Word. They had embraced the "church-as-usual" lie. But believers were never created for church-as-usual. We were created for the supernatural!

SUPERNATURAL RECREATION

The next end-time move of God will be too momentous to be referred to as either a revival or a reformation. This move of the Spirit will be what I call a *supernatural recreation*. God will change the fabric of the spiritual DNA of the church and believers everywhere. No more will we settle for less than what the Bible promises us. No more will the world disregard the church's authority and influence in the earth because we will be actively demonstrating God's kingdom. No more will our churches and hospitals be filled with sick people because healing will flow. There will not be a commingling of religious tradition and grace as there was in the early Protestant Reformation, where many of the monks and religious leaders still functioned according to the same religious ideologies while wearing a mask of grace. There will be a complete change.

WHAT DOES IT MEAN FOR YOU TO BE THE SALT OF THE EARTH AND THE LIGHT OF WORLD?

Jesus said that we are *"the salt of the earth"* (Matthew 5:13) and *"the light of the world"* (verse 14), and it is high time that we became salt and light. Once we have embraced the newness of life that the Holy Spirit came to give us, we will no longer vacillate between the world and the church. That is not the type of life that Jesus Christ shed His blood for.

This will be a supernatural recreation of the very foundation of our perception of God, ourselves, and other people! When we are recreated in the very image of God, it will not be difficult for us to love others. When the young people in our churches are exposed to the pure Word of God, they will be completely sold out for Jesus Christ. They will no longer backslide during their college years. They will not become caught up in premarital sex or drugs. There will be no more spiritual wilderness experiences—only an experience of God's love and power.

My desire is to provoke you to jealousy by telling you what is actually available to you compared to what you might be experiencing right now. There is a stirring deep down inside of your spirit for more. You have prayed, fasted, and asked questions, but now it is time to enter into the fullness of what God has to offer! You were created for God's glory and power to be manifested through you. You were created to be a doorway to His supernatural anointing. You are meant to stand up with spiritual power and authority to defeat the enemy. We will show the world how real God is by living as the new creations in Christ that He has made us to be.

YOU WERE CREATED TO BE A DOORWAY TO GOD'S SUPERNATURAL ANOINTING.

VICTORY PRAYER

Father, in the name of Jesus, I recognize that I am recreated in the image of Christ Jesus and that, by design, I am called and commissioned to carry Your supernatural power. Thank You for including me in the end-time move of the Spirit to bring the revelation of who You are to others around me. Right now, I receive a supernatural download of new-creation power, which will enable me to think like You, speak like You, and operate like You! I will no longer settle for church-as-usual, but I will absorb the reality of Your kingdom into every area of my life. Thank You for releasing Your supernatural power through me!

UNLOCKING THE CODE OF THE SUPERNATURAL INSIGHTS

1. Why did the Protestant Reformation take place?

2. What was a major drawback of the Reformation?

3. What does the Greek word *ktizo*, translated as *"created"* in Colossians 3:10, reveal about what it means for us to be made new by God?

4. What will the next end-time move of God be like?

MIRACLE TESTIMONY

AN ANGELIC VISITATION

One night, I had an angelic visitation. I awoke from sleep and saw an angel staring at me with the most perplexed look on his face. It was as if he was bewildered by the notion that God would spend such effort and resources on "little ol' me." The angel didn't say anything; he just kept gazing. However, it was as if we were having a full conversation. The word that came to mind was *rest*. At that time, I was very discouraged by the persecution I had been experiencing from other believers. I was encouraged by this encounter, and, when I woke up the next day, I had fresh zeal and enthusiasm for the things of God.

10

WILL YOU BE MADE WHOLE?

*"Now there is at Jerusalem by the sheep market a pool, which is called
in the Hebrew tongue Bethesda, having five porches.
In these lay a great multitude of impotent folk, of blind, halt,
withered, waiting for the moving of the water. For an angel went
down at a certain season into the pool, and troubled the water:
whosoever then first after the troubling of the water stepped in was
made whole of whatsoever disease he had. And a certain man was
there, which had an infirmity thirty and eight years. When Jesus saw
him lie, and knew that he had been now a long time in that case,
He says to him, Will you be made whole?"*
—John 5:2–6

In John 5, there is a very interesting account of Jesus's interaction with a man who had been lame for thirty-eight years. I believe this scenario speaks volumes regarding the state of the church at large (and humanity in general). I often look at this story as a representation of the church because many believers are in a similar state of infirmity—both spiritually and physically. There are men and women who have been bound for years by fear, feelings of condemnation, physical or emotional sickness, addiction, and a host of other oppressive mindsets.

This man at the Pool of Bethesda had given up on having a life that transcended what he believed to be an unchangeable situation. He responded to Jesus's question, "*Will you be made whole?*" by saying, "*Sir, I have no man, when the water is troubled, to put me into the pool: but while I am coming, another steps down before me*" (John 5:7). The man had become a victim due to his oppressive situation. And his focus was now on other people providing for his well-being.

This is what happens when we are living beneath the potential God has given us in Christ. We look for circumstances and even external moves of God in which to place our confidence. Consequently, we say things like, "One day, God is going to change my situation" or "One day, I will overcome!" when the reality is that God has given us everything we need as new creations to live the life that He has ordained for us. In fact, this illustration in the gospel of John perfectly depicts the salvation process. The invalid man was bound and in desperate need of salvation. We must remember that salvation is more than saying a prayer to accept Jesus Christ, but it involves a holistic deliverance of spirit, mind, and body.

If a fireman were to rescue someone from a burning building and then simply leave them on the side of the road suffering from smoke inhalation and second-degree burns, we could not really say that the person was saved. The negative effects of having been injured in the fire would continue to pose an imminent threat to their well-being. As long as those issues remained unaddressed, the person's life would still be in danger. Likewise, in a spiritual sense, to be saved, it is not enough to separate ourselves from negative situations and behaviors; we need to be made whole.

Jesus graciously offered the infirm man the opportunity to be everything God intended him to be. Again, this is a perfect picture of what takes place in redemption. Note that the first question the Lord asked was, "**Will** *you be made whole?*" This question is very important because it lets us know that living in victory involves our will. God wants us to desire His will for our lives. He wants us to fully embrace the plan He set in motion in eternity past. This plan is for us to be new creations and to be conformed to the image of Jesus. He asks the same question of us: "Will you be made whole?"

In this incident, Jesus was looking at one of His creations and seeing a life that was insufficient and void, all because the man didn't realize there was so much more for him in God. He didn't realize that his wholeness was not dependent on other people or even religious practices. It was contingent upon his personal revelation of the unlimited power of Jesus Christ.

Jesus gave three commands to the man: *"Rise, take up your bed, and walk"* (John 5:8). Once we understand and apply these commands, they will transform our lives forever. Let's look at each statement, noting how it corresponds to a particular dimension of our triune being.

RISE! (SPIRIT)

When Jesus told the man to *"rise,"* it indicated more than just a physical movement from one position to another. In John 5:8, the Greek word translated *"rise"* is *egeiro*, which means "to arouse, cause to rise." It can signify the idea of "to arouse from the sleep of death, to recall the dead to life." It denotes a calling forth out of a state of spiritual and physical slumber or death. I believe the word *"rise"* represents salvation from a degenerate, dead spiritual state.

Thus, spiritually speaking, the man at the Pool of Bethesda was dead. He was lying near the pool of mercy, but he was unresponsive to the presence and power of God to change his situation. Ephesians 2:1 says, *"And you has He quickened, who were dead in trespasses and sins."* When Jesus called the man to rise, He was awakening him from spiritual death. God did the same for us who believe in Christ. When we heard the gospel for the first time, God called us by His grace into a new life. He extended the invitation to come out of spiritual slumber and death. This is the essence of the new birth. We were bound near our own Pool of Bethesda, having a form of godliness but no power. We were dead in our trespasses and sins. But we heard the gospel of grace, which is pregnant with the miracle-working power of God. We received the faith to believe (through the gospel), and we responded to the grace of almighty God by repenting of our sins and accepting the lordship of Jesus Christ.

It is critical for us to understand that the Word of God contains life-giving power. I believe that the word Jesus spoke to this man was filled with God's omnipotent power to enable him to rise up. Oh, may the church embrace the truth that we do not rely on our own strength or good works but on the strength of God's sovereign Word!

THE WORD OF GOD CONTAINS LIFE-GIVING POWER.

In the presence of the Christ, the infirm man had no more religious excuses to lean on, no more reasons for why he had to remain in his weak condition, no more explanations for why he was not being what God intended him to be. He could no longer blame his parents for not rearing him correctly or his spouse for hurting him. He was in the presence of unlimited power and mercy and was being called to deliverance and healing in a way he never dreamed possible.

HOW DO YOU RESPOND TO JESUS'S QUESTION,

"WILL YOU BE MADE WHOLE?"

114 Unlocking the Code of the Supernatural

Would he be made whole? Would he accept the offer that was on the eternal table? This was the real issue! Jesus's command to *"rise"* gives us deep insight into what is available to us today if we would only respond to His call. Again, this is not just a call to material success in life and ministry, but a call to victory in every area that concerns us. This is salvation! This is the redemption we received when we gave our hearts to Jesus. Our spiritual DNA was changed from death to life, from carnal to spiritual. The life of the Almighty began to flow in and through us from that moment.

The question is, where do we go from here? We "take up our bed"!

TAKE UP YOUR BED! (SOUL)

When Jesus commanded the man at the Pool of Bethesda to rise, He also told him, *"Take up your bed."* What does this statement imply? It masterfully illustrates Jesus's true intent for the man—and for us today. The Greek word translated as *"take up"* is *airo*, which means "to raise up, elevate, lift up." Jesus commanded the lame man to physically take up his bed, but there was so much more in that word.

Airo can also mean "to take upon one's self and carry what has been raised up." From a spiritual perspective, Jesus's word had already raised the man up, but he had to appropriate that word in order to make it a physical reality. Simply put, the man had a part to play! It was not enough for him to hear the command of Jesus—he had to participate in it. This participation represents sanctification in the life of the believer. Sanctification is the process of consecrating something for holy purposes. The Greek word for "sanctification" is *hagiasmos*, which means "consecration, purification." In various passages in the King James Version, this word is translated as either "holiness" or "sanctification."

As we go through the process of sanctification, we align our external life with our internal life. We appropriate the spiritual reality into a physical reality. This process requires the renewal of our minds. In Romans 12:1–2, Paul exclaims:

> *I beseech you therefore, brethren, by the mercies of God, that you present your bodies a living sacrifice, holy, acceptable to God, which is your reasonable service. And be not conformed to this world: but be you*

transformed by the renewing of your mind, that you may prove what is that good, and acceptable, and perfect, will of God.

We need to change the way we think and reason to correspond with God's Word. Without such a transformation, we won't be able to fully embrace all that Jesus has accomplished for us. Countless Christians have said a prayer of salvation but don't have a life that lines up with that profession because they haven't changed the way they think. We have to play a part in our sanctification process. We have to decide that we don't want to remain in our former condition any longer.

Remember that God has already elevated us into the spiritual realm. We are seated with Jesus in *"heavenly places"*: *"[God] has raised us up together, and made us sit together in heavenly places in Christ Jesus"* (Ephesians 2:6). The phrase *"raised us up together"* is translated from the Greek word *synegeiro*, one of whose roots is the word for *"rise"* in John 5:8. In essence, we have been raised by the power of God's Spirit. We are not in the same position we were in before. The challenge for us is in *believing* this truth. But the moment we embrace this reality, our life is set apart. It takes on new meaning and purpose.

Therefore, sanctification is not just behavioral modification. It is not following dos and don'ts. It is coming to the realization that we have already been raised together with Christ and made to sit together with Him in the heavenly places. It is the unveiling of a life charged with God's supernatural power. That is why we can never be the same from the moment of our salvation.

AS WE GO THROUGH THE PROCESS OF SANCTIFICATION, WE ALIGN OUR EXTERNAL LIFE WITH OUR INTERNAL LIFE. WE APPROPRIATE THE SPIRITUAL REALITY INTO A PHYSICAL REALITY.

Some people may ask, "Isn't sanctification an act of God's grace?" The answer is yes! However, this fact doesn't imply that we do not have a personal responsibility in the process. As a matter of fact, Jesus goes out of His way to show us how much responsibility we have. He told the man to "take up his bed." To the casual Bible reader, this may not seem like a significant detail, but when we examine it more closely through the eyes of a Jew in ancient Palestine, we can see that there was more to it.

During that time, sick people in Jerusalem were typically poor and often confined to a bed. The Greek word translated *"bed"* in John 5:8 is *krabattos*. The word refers to "a pallet, camp bed (a rather simple bed holding only one person)." This type of bed was a sick person's home. It was essentially their permanent residence. It was how they identified themselves because, in that culture, the bed of affliction indicated to everyone around them what type of problem they had.

Jesus did not take up the bed for this man; He wanted the man to do it himself. This incident represents a complete act of God's grace and mercy, as well as our need to take ownership over our deliverance and the outworking of our salvation. Philippians 2:12 says, *"Wherefore, my beloved, as you have always obeyed, not as in my presence only, but now much more in my absence, work out your own salvation with fear and trembling."* We are responsible for working out what God has already worked in. Jesus did not want the man to identify himself as a victim any longer. He wanted him to be empowered.

This mindset is the opposite of modern-day, victim-based Christianity, which tells you how much of a wretch you are. Religion is all about reminding you of how useless you are apart from God. However, the problem with this way of thinking is that it neglects this truth: if you are born again, you are no longer apart from God! Through Christ Jesus, you are one with the Father. Therefore, you are no longer useless and wretched, but you are empowered and enabled by God to live the way He intended. No more bed of affliction for you! Take up your bed of hindrance today. Take ownership and authority over your thoughts and attitudes by actively renewing your mind.

Where do we go from here? We walk!

WALK! (NATURAL LIFE)

Jesus's final instruction to the lame man was to *"walk."* Now, this word is self-explanatory, right? Actually, it is loaded with powerful truth. Notice that Jesus did not say, "Rise, take up your bed, and get in the pool!" Why didn't He say that?

The pool represents past religious experiences. In effect, if Jesus had commanded the man to get into the pool, He would have caused him to continue to be dependent on a religious system. Jumping into the pool would not have required any change in his thinking, any renewal of his mind. The infirm man would never have acknowledged that the Word of God was what he needed to live life to the full.

Thus, instead of allowing the man to retain a sense of dependency on the Pool of Bethesda, Jesus told him to move on to something better. The word *"walk"* is translated from the Greek term *peripateo*, one definition of which is "to make one's way, progress; to make due use of opportunities." Although the man's healing was an instantaneous miracle, the implication was for him to continuously move forward. Jesus was not merely calling him to a life of natural progress but also to a life filled with the supernatural power of God. He was calling this man to walk in the supernatural! Similarly, we have been called by God to move forward in the power of the Spirit to manifest His kingdom.

Isn't it good news that God desires to demonstrate His love and favor through us? He wants us to walk this thing out! When Jesus uttered the word *"walk,"* His word became spirit and life to this "dead" man, who was then empowered to carry out God's original intent for his life. (See John 6:63.) Beloved, God is saying the same thing to us today—He is telling us to *walk*. He does not want us to perch beside the pool of religious works, the pool of the past, or the pool of apathy. The mystery of this command to walk is that the more we act on God's Word, the more confident we become in His power and the more we progress in our spiritual lives, demonstrating that power.

Being a believer in Jesus is not about being ordinary. We are not to live a life of mediocrity. We are called to live a life pregnant with the supernatural. After this man accepted Jesus's word and received his healing, wherever he walked, he was a living testament to the power of Christ. He was fulfilling the truths we read about in Romans 12:2:

And be not conformed to this world: but be you transformed by the renewing of your mind, that you may prove what is that good, and acceptable, and perfect, will of God.

The Greek word for *"prove"* here is *dokimazo,* which means "to test, examine, prove, scrutinize (to see whether a thing is genuine or not), as metals to recognize as genuine after examination, to approve, deem worthy." We are called by God to present our bodies as living sacrifices that are acceptable to God. Our lives ought to be witnesses to the resurrection power of Jesus Christ.

IN WHAT WAYS IS YOUR LIFE A WITNESS TO JESUS'S RESURRECTION POWER?

In Romans 8:13–14, Paul wrote:

For if you live after the flesh, you shall die: but if you through the Spirit do mortify the deeds of the body, you shall live. For as many as are led by the Spirit of God, they are the sons of God.

You must ask yourself these very important questions: Is my life exemplifying the power that raised Jesus from the dead? Do people receive an impartation of the victorious Spirit of God from me? Are people challenged to live at a higher level of spiritual life because of me? Are people convinced that they can live a life free from sin because of my testimony? If your answer to any of these questions is no, then there is so much of the life of the Spirit that you are neglecting.

When we get up and walk in the power of God, we take dominion over every attack of the enemy. We tread on every obstacle and excuse the devil can concoct. We no longer ask God, "Please don't pass me by," but we say, "Lord, please demonstrate Your kingdom through me!" Christ's victory expanded beyond the man's spirit and soul into the natural realm of his life. Walking represented the final dimension to be conquered. It was the final expression of the restoring power of God. Like this man, we have been commissioned by God to walk out His "super" in our natural. He wants us to demonstrate to the fallen world around us that His power is truly omnipotent!

THE MORE WE ACT ON GOD'S WORD, THE MORE CONFIDENT WE BECOME IN HIS POWER AND THE MORE WE PROGRESS IN OUR SPIRITUAL LIVES, DEMONSTRATING THAT POWER.

VICTORY PRAYER

Father, in the name of Jesus Christ, I recognize that it is Your will for me to be whole in every area of my life. Right now, I receive wholeness in my spirit, soul, and body. I declare that I have been made complete. Today, I decide to renew my mind through the Word of God. Father, please demonstrate Your kingdom through me! I receive supernatural empowerment by Your Spirit to live out Your original intent for my life. I *"mortify the deeds of the body"* through the power of your indwelling Spirit. Fear, anger, and bitterness no longer control me. In Jesus's name, amen!

UNLOCKING THE CODE OF THE SUPERNATURAL INSIGHTS

1. What is the spiritual significance of Jesus's command to rise?

2. What does it mean for us to "take up our bed"?

3. Why did Jesus tell the infirm man to walk rather than to step into the Pool of Bethesda?

4. How should we "walk forward" in life as new creations in Christ?

11

OLD THINGS HAVE PASSED AWAY

*"Therefore if any man be in Christ, he is a new creature: old things
are passed away; behold, all things are become new."*
—2 Corinthians 5:17

There is a simple spiritual truth that is somehow very difficult for us to
accept: *"old things are passed away."* Many believers with a religious mindset
attempt to embrace their new life but fail to grasp the spiritual reality that,
from God's perspective, their old life is no more. Most people's hang-ups
involve negative past experiences because they are often the origin of our
feelings of guilt, shame, and condemnation.

INTERNAL TATTOOS

Earlier, I used a hypothetical illustration about a person who was an
idol worshipper and had idolatrous tattoos on their skin, but then gave
their life to Jesus Christ. The individual's tattoos would not automatically
be erased once they became a believer. So, even though that person would
be brand-new on the inside, they would not necessarily appear new out-
wardly, whether in their appearance or, to some extent, their behavior. This
might cause others to be judgmental of them.

Those physical tattoos represent the person's *past* negative attitudes, choices, and failures. But most people have a tendency to judge others by their external features without recognizing, or seeking to learn, the character of their inner self. In a similar way, many believers in the church are branding themselves by what I call "internal tattoos," or thoughts about their sinful past. Satan uses people's memories of these negative experiences to manipulate them into trying to perform in order to earn God's love, acceptance, and validation. Sadly, in addition to the fact that Satan stands in the corridors of our churches every Sunday to accuse Christians, he receives much assistance from their fellow believers! We live in a culture where people are too often affirmed or disqualified based on their pasts. Consequently, most people try to either hide their pasts or manipulate other people's perception of them. Meanwhile, they judge themselves for their mistakes and shortcomings.

Why is it so difficult for us to accept the fact that if we are born-again children of God, our pasts have been wiped away? One reason is that we live in a world where we are constantly reminded of people's pasts. News articles and gossip shows thrive on reporting the embarrassments and misdeeds of public figures, including religious leaders. When political candidates run against each other, one of their primary methods of advancing their political chances is to discover and reveal as much "dirt" on the opposing candidate as possible.

Regretfully, the church has taken a similar approach. We attempt to validate our own denominations or specific doctrinal positions by trying to discredit those who differ from us. Therefore, one of the major reasons why we find it hard to accept the truth that our history is no longer a factor in our relationship with God is that we have made a habit of holding ourselves and others hostage to the past.

Have you ever been in a conversation in which someone brings up another person's former failings as a means of "disqualifying" them from approval and acceptance? Have you ever heard a pastor or Christian leader reveal the failings of another Christian leader, perhaps to make themselves look better in comparison? This satanically inspired culture in the church aids and abets a spirit of paralyzing guilt and condemnation that

is prevalent today. However, we must accept the authority of the Word of God on this matter above any other influence.

The reality is that all of us have areas in our lives in which we have sinned, and about which we are not proud. I am not saying there aren't times when appropriate church discipline is necessary for leaders and other believers if they have committed wrongs. The Bible teaches there are specific qualifications for leadership and holy living. When people step outside of the boundaries God has set forth, they should be corrected in love. However, that is not the point I am addressing here. I'm referring to what happens when we allow what God has already cleansed from our lives to keep us from accepting His love and walking according to His Spirit—and when we judge others for their past wrongs.

HAVE YOU BEEN JUDGING YOURSELF FOR YOUR PAST MISTAKES AND SINS? HOW DOES GOD WANT YOU TO THINK ABOUT THEM?

OUR OLD NATURE HAS PERISHED!

Let's now look more closely at Paul's statement *"old things are passed away."* The Greek word translated *"old things"* is *archaios*, which can signify "original, primal, old, ancient." What is the implication of this phrase for us? *"Old things"* refers to the original nature, or the sinful nature, we possessed apart from Christ. The word rendered *"passed away"* is *parerchomai*, which means "to pass away, perish." When we put these two ideas together, we see that our old nature has indeed perished. It has been abolished. It is no more!

Wow! Really? Are you telling me that the "old me" doesn't exist anymore? Absolutely! The truth is, the only thing that keeps the past alive for us is our thoughts about it. We were crucified with Christ before we were made alive in Him; therefore, our old nature is dead. Yet, in a large number of churches, the content of the songs, hymns, and teachings effectively attempts to resurrect the old nature in people. We use adjectives like these to describe Christians: *weak, wretched, poor, broken, lost, sinful*. However, none of these words should be used as depictions of believers. There is no nobility in being "wretched" after you have become a Christian. As a matter of fact, if you are still wretched after being saved, it is not a very good witness to the change that has taken place within you. Christ came to set us free from our wretchedness.

WE ARE AMBASSADORS FOR CHRIST

In 2 Corinthians 5:20, Paul writes, *"Now then we are ambassadors for Christ, as though God did beseech you by us: we pray you in Christ's stead, be you reconciled to God."* Believers are emissaries of God's kingdom. We are called by Him to represent all things new in Christ. We are couriers of the mystery of the new nature. In fact, this is the primary ministry of every believer. Before we are called to be apostles, prophets, evangelist, pastors, or teachers; before we are called to exercise any spiritual gift, we are called to be Christ's ambassadors. Our lives are meant to be windows into the heavenly realm, embodying the new life in its fullness. We are not just religious followers displaying our piety. We are people who have been redeemed from the old and translated by the Spirit of God into the new.

This is why Satan insidiously uses the past to attempt to control us. If the enemy can keep us focused on our sins, mistakes, and failures, he can successfully prevent us from walking as ambassadors of Christ.

RECONCILED TO GOD

The question is, what does it mean that the old nature has passed away? Paul proclaims the profound answer in 2 Corinthians 5:18: *"And all things are of God, who has reconciled us to Himself by Jesus Christ, and has given to us the ministry of reconciliation."* Our new life is an existence in which God has reconciled us to Himself. The idea in the original Greek is that of a merchant engaging in a monetary transaction to purchase a slave's freedom. God Himself, in Christ, paid the penalty of our past so He could have a restored, intimate relationship with us. He paid the price for our guilt and shame so that we no longer have to live under slave conditions. We are free to worship Him—not through our own sacrifice but through His sacrifice.

OUR LIVES ARE MEANT TO BE WINDOWS INTO THE HEAVENLY REALM, EMBODYING THE NEW LIFE IN ITS FULLNESS.

This means that our lives are liberated from bondage to the past. We have been given permission by God to live guilt-free. Is it really possible to live in this way? The answer is an emphatic *yes!* We can have lives that are filled with God's power and love. We can have lives that are free from the condemnation of the past. The moment we embrace this spiritual reality, the devil is powerless against our future.

GOD CAN'T REMEMBER!

The Word of God affirms that we have been forgiven and cleansed from our old life. It doesn't matter what Satan, society, or other Christians have to say about it. If we have come to Jesus in sincere repentance, then our past is no more. We no longer have to be enslaved by our former failures, sins, and struggles. Did you know the Bible says that God has cast our sins into the depths of the sea? (See Micah 7:19.) Scripture also says that He will no longer even *remember* our sins. If you don't believe me, read this:

For I will be merciful to their unrighteousness, and their sins and their iniquities will I remember no more.
                                   —Hebrews 8:12; see also Jeremiah 31:31–34

God has the sovereign ability to cause Himself to forget. Oh, if only we would imitate our heavenly Father and learn to forget the past, I believe we would have a much more successful Christian experience. God does not remember your sin anymore. So, I am so sorry to break it to you, but you have been forgiven!

It is as if we believe that forgetting the past makes us weak or irresponsible. Beloved, it does not! God has made a covenant with us through Christ that He will no longer remember our sins. We have often been taught that God is pleased when we tell Him how sinful we are, but the truth is that God doesn't even know what we are talking about! We go to the Lord and say, "God, I just want to let You know that I am such a wretched, poor, wicked, deceitful, drug-dealing, prostituting, hypocritical, horrible sinner saved by grace, and I am sorry for all my sins." God replies, "What sins? I don't remember them!"

Sadly, even as we talk about God's grace and mercy in our lives, we are afraid to believe the parts of the Bible that say we are forgiven. The purpose of His grace and mercy is to both exonerate us of our sin and empower us to walk in righteousness. We are not supposed to wallow in the guilt of the past. Paul the apostle expressed this revelation in his epistle to the Philippians:

Brethren, I count not myself to have apprehended: but this one thing I do, forgetting those things which are behind, and reaching forth to those things which are before, I press toward the mark for the prize of the high calling of God in Christ Jesus.   —Philippians 3:13–14

Paul says, "*This one thing I do.*" In essence, he is saying, "If there is anything that is important for me to invest my time and energy in, it is this: forgetting!" He boldly declares that he is going to forget his past. As a matter of fact, Paul uses the Greek word *epilanthanomai*, one definition of which is "given over to oblivion, i.e. uncared for." Paul was saying that his past is no longer a part of his spiritual equation. He does not factor it in anymore. It no longer exists.

Remember that this passage was written by someone who, prior to his conversion, murdered Jewish believers in Jesus. Paul understood Satan's deceptive plans. He had enough experience as a believer to pinpoint the enemy's attempt to use his past to neutralize his ministry. Again, there are so many believers today who have been rendered ineffective by the enemy because they are living in the past. They may have had a moral failure or been divorced, and the enemy has spoken to them just as he spoke to Eve in the garden of Eden: he has seduced them into believing they need to open themselves to the knowledge of good and evil in the sense of looking outside of their relationship with God for affirmation. Unfortunately, they have believed the lie that, because of their failings, they are no longer useful to God.

WHAT SIN IN YOUR PAST WILL YOU RELEASE TODAY, KNOWING THAT GOD HAS "CAST IT INTO THE DEPTHS OF THE SEA" AND NO LONGER REMEMBERS IT?

The apostle Paul knew better, and we ought to know better too. Our past does not determine our future. We have a bright and glorious future because of Christ Jesus! God does not want us to be stuck in our past. He wants us to forget our failings, just as He has.

Paul not only forgets his past, but he also puts it behind him. The Greek word for *"behind"* in Philippians 3:13 is *opiso*, which means "back, behind, after, afterwards." The implication is that our past should be at our back. We should never move in the direction of our past, only our future. A good illustration of this truth is the way a sprinter runs a race. Runners must move in the direction of the finish line at all times. Once their foot leaves the starting line, they cannot look back for any reason but must continue progressing forward until they reach the finish. If they look back, it will slow them down, which could cost them the race.

Similarly, as believers, we cannot afford to look back at the past for any reason. If we do, then we are not going to be able to move toward our goal, and that goal is to please God. In Philippians, Paul says that his strategy is to *"press toward the mark"* (verse 14). The Greek word rendered *"press"* is *dioko*, which can mean "to run swiftly in order to catch a person or thing, to run after," "to press on: figuratively of one who in a race runs swiftly to reach the goal," and "to pursue." This is the attitude we should possess. We are to drive away any thought, influence, or idea that is contrary to our goal of finishing the race God has set before us. We must be determined to walk in the fullness of the Spirit. We cannot settle for anything less than a new life in Christ Jesus. What good is it to go to church on a regular basis but never experience the newness God has ordained?

A NEW AND BETTER COVENANT

God has made a covenant with us that includes specific and tangible blessings. Isn't it encouraging to know that we are under a new covenant with Him? If we are going to walk in the power and authority of our new nature, we must understand the ramifications of this covenant. There seems to be much debate in the church today about the implications of the new covenant. Some believers erroneously think that the freedom of their new relationship with God excuses them from the need to exercise integrity and be spiritually accountable. Others still subscribe to a legalistic interpretation of Christianity, as if they remain subject to the old covenant.

So, what is the nature of the new covenant? What has God given us? The covenant God has established with us exceeds anything we could ever imagine in the natural realm. It goes far beyond religion and tradition into a supernatural world that many Christians have yet to explore.

In Hebrews 8:6–10, the Bible declares:

But now has He [Jesus] obtained a more excellent ministry, by how much also He is the mediator of a better covenant, which was established upon better promises. For if that first covenant had been faultless, then should no place have been sought for the second. For finding fault with them, He says, Behold, the days come, says the Lord, when I will make a new covenant with the house of Israel and with the house of Judah: not according to the covenant that I made with their fathers in the day when I took them by the hand to lead them out of the land of Egypt; because they continued not in My covenant, and I regarded them not, says the Lord. For this is the covenant that I will make with the house of Israel after those days, says the Lord; I will put My laws into their mind, and write them in their hearts: and I will be to them a God, and they shall be to Me a people.

We have been given a new covenant that is *"established upon better promises."* This is good news for the body of Christ. At least, it should be good news! However, many believers are ignorant of these *"better promises,"* which is why they are still approaching God according to an old-covenant paradigm. Hebrews 8 tells us that God found fault with the first covenant. It is not that the covenant was faulty in itself. However, the fact is, it could not save anyone! God wrestled with the Israelites for many years, but they still could not come into the fullness of the covenant that He had made with their forefathers Abraham, Isaac, and Jacob. The reason was that the covenant God made with the Israelites could not be fulfilled based on the law; it had to be carried out through a Mediator.

GOD HAS ESTABLISHED A COVENANT WITH US THAT FAR EXCEEDS ANYTHING WE COULD EVER IMAGINE IN THE NATURAL REALM.

The Mediator of the new covenant is Jesus Christ. If we are going to continue unfolding the mystery of our new nature, then we must truly understand the difference between the covenants. Under the old covenant, God dealt with the children of Israel based upon their ability to keep His laws and ordinances. A system of sacrifices was established to atone for the people's sins when they violated those laws and ordinances. For this reason, under that system, there was always a remembrance of sin. For example, we read in Leviticus 23:27:

Also on the tenth day of this seventh month there shall be a day of atonement: it shall be a holy convocation to you; and you shall afflict your souls, and offer an offering made by fire to the LORD.

Today, this yearly convocation is commonly known as Yom Kippur or the Day of Atonement. It was a time of remembering and accounting for all of the sins the people had committed in the previous year. God instructed the Israelites to *"afflict"* their souls. What did this mean? They were to humble themselves in the Lord's presence in repentance for their trespasses, iniquities, and transgressions.

To offer the sacrifice of atonement, the high priest would take two goats and cast lots to determine which goat would be the offering and which would be the scapegoat. The priest would sacrifice one goat as a sin offering to the Lord and sprinkle its blood on the mercy seat of the ark of the covenant. Then, he would lay his hands on the scapegoat, transferring all of the Israelites' sin onto it and releasing it into the wilderness, symbolizing the putting away of the people's sins that year. (See Leviticus 16.)

Yearly atonement had to be made for both the high priest and the people. Why was this atonement necessary? The Israelites would sin throughout the year, and provision had to made for these sins to be forgiven. The blood on the mercy seat symbolized God's compassion on His people.

Thus, in Israel, there was a continual remembrance of sin, and this reminder characterized the old covenant. God wanted the people to recognize they had violated the covenant and laws He had given them. He wanted them to remember their wrongs so they could repent of them. The Day of Atonement was such a serious convocation that if anyone violated God's ordinances on that day, that person would be cut off from Israel. (See Leviticus 23:29.)

Atonement has a different significance under the new covenant. There is no need for a yearly sacrifice because Christ the Messiah has become both our sin offering and our scapegoat. He took our place! In His sacrifice, the sin of the world was laid on Him, the wrath of God punished that sin, and Christ's blood was shed to permanently wash away our iniquities. We no longer need to have a continual consciousness of sin.

We still need to repent when we do wrong, but because of the Messiah's sacrifice, we are no longer under God's judgment for sin. When we sin, we can confess our transgression to God and immediately receive His forgiveness so we can move forward again. *"If we confess our sins, He is faithful and just to forgive us our sins, and to cleanse us from all unrighteousness"* (1 John 1:9). Under the old covenant, an imperfect high priest sacrificed for himself and the rest of the people every year. In contrast, under the new covenant, Jesus Christ is our perfect High Priest who sacrificed Himself once and for all, and His blood continues to testify on our behalf on the heavenly mercy seat. Under the new covenant, the death of One has made many righteous. (See Romans 5:19.) Isn't it exciting news that Christ was sacrificed for us once and for all?

Oh, we ought to be excited about that fact! God has made a better covenant with us. He no longer remembers our sins. Again, if God no longer remembers our sins, then we shouldn't either. The promise of this new covenant is eternal life. And this eternal life is not just for the hereafter; it flows in us right now because our High Priest and Sacrifice dwells within us! This is what empowers us to walk victoriously.

> JESUS CHRIST IS OUR PERFECT HIGH PRIEST WHO SACRIFICED HIMSELF ONCE AND FOR ALL, AND HIS BLOOD CONTINUES TO TESTIFY ON OUR BEHALF ON THE HEAVENLY MERCY SEAT.

Additionally, the writer of Hebrews, quoting Jeremiah 31, records that God says, *"I will put My laws into their mind, and write them in their hearts: and I will be to them a God, and they shall be to Me a people"* (Hebrews 8:10). We no longer have to follow external rules and regulations because a knowledge of God and His ways has been placed inside of us! Through this knowledge, we identify with God as our Father and do what is pleasing to Him. I don't know what the enemy has been telling you lately, but, right now, I announce to you that God is your Father and you are His child! It is time for you to walk in this identity. You are no longer your past. Instead, you are a new creation, and you are everything God says you are as His beloved son or daughter!

VICTORY PRAYER

Father, I thank You for the eternal, atoning sacrifice of Your Son Jesus. I thank You that my sins have been washed away and cast into the depths of the sea. From this day forward, I recognize that You no longer remember my past sins. Therefore, I no longer remember my past sins either! I embrace the full magnitude of the new covenant. I live under a better covenant than that of the Old Testament patriarchs. Everywhere I go and every person I meet is an opportunity for me to represent the kingdom of God, and I walk in my assignment as an ambassador of Christ. In the name of Jesus Christ, I pray. Amen!

UNLOCKING THE CODE OF THE SUPERNATURAL INSIGHTS

1. What does the Bible say God does with our sins when we have sincerely repented of them?

2. What is God's "memory" of our sins?

3. What is the purpose of God's grace and mercy?

4. What is the difference between the old covenant and the new covenant?

12

LIVING FROM THE INSIDE OUT

"And when He had called all the people to Him, He said to them, Hearken to Me every one of you, and understand: there is nothing from outside a man, that entering into him can defile him: but the things which come out of him, those are they that defile the man. If any man have ears to hear, let him hear.... For from inside, out of the heart of men, proceed evil thoughts, adulteries, fornications, murders, thefts, covetousness, wickedness, deceit, lasciviousness, an evil eye, blasphemy, pride, foolishness: all these evil things come from inside, and defile the man."
—Mark 7:14–16, 21–23

"A good man out of the good treasure of the heart brings forth good things: and an evil man out of the evil treasure brings forth evil things."
—Matthew 12:35

Transformation begins from the inside out, not the outside in. Religion focuses on the outward person, but true Christianity deals with the inner person. Jesus addressed this issue in the gospel of Mark when the Pharisees accused His disciples of eating without ceremonially washing their hands. To an untrained onlooker, it might seem as if the religious leaders had a legitimate concern because it was a common tradition of the day to engage in this ritualistic cleansing. Jesus knew better. The issue was not about keeping a tradition but rather about religious control. The Pharisees prided themselves on looking the part. They had the right garments, the right education, the right ceremonies, the right speech, and even the right walk, but they were dead on the inside.

WORKING OUT OUR SALVATION

Earlier in this book, we talked about Jesus's conversation with Nicodemus in which He told the Pharisee that he must be born again. Once more, until our inner nature is transformed—and until we live out that transformation—we will find it impossible to carry out the purpose and plan of God for our lives. You may ask, "Is it really possible to change from the inside out?" It is not only possible, but it is required! Here is what the Word of God says in the book of Philippians:

Wherefore, my beloved, as you have always obeyed, not as in my presence only, but now much more in my absence, work out your own salvation with fear and trembling. For it is God which works in you both to will and to do of His good pleasure.
—Philippians 2:12–13

As we can clearly see from Paul's exhortation to the Philippian believers, working out our salvation is not something God gives us as an option; it is imperative! We are required by God to work out our own salvation as the Lord works His will and power within us.

In previous chapters, I have talked about some of my experiences growing up in the church. These experiences included an involvement in the holiness movement. This particular movement focused on holy living as the ethos of the Christian message, and this lifestyle included refraining from certain behaviors and activities. For example, if you were a woman, you were encouraged not to wear makeup or even jewelry. The idea was to avoid worldliness and drawing attention to yourself. However, an emphasis on external matters led many people in this movement to essentially try to work out their salvation through outward actions and to overlook the essential gospel message.

I praise God for some of the positive aspects of the holiness tradition, but an external focus is not what Paul was talking about in Philippians 2:12 when he exhorted believers to work out their salvation. To understand this biblical concept, we must combine it with the truths found in verse 13: *"For it is God which works in you both to will and to do of His good pleasure."* The Greek word translated *"works"* is *energeo*, which means "to be operative, be at work, put forth power." This is amazing! It is God's power operating in us that enables us to carry out His good pleasure.

HOW MIGHT YOU BE TRYING TO LIVE YOUR CHRISTIAN LIFE FROM THE OUTSIDE IN, RATHER THAN THE INSIDE OUT?

When I was younger, I would often hear the expression, "It takes God to love God." This is actually a very scriptural idea. The fact is, unless God is working in us, we cannot do His good pleasure. True holiness comes from within us. So, when Paul says that we should work out our own salvation, he is really telling us to work out what God has already worked in. The Greek word for *"work out"* in Philippians 2:12 is *katergazomai*, which means "to perform, accomplish, achieve" and "to work out, i.e., to do that from which something results."

Therefore, God wants us to manifest what He has already deposited inside of us. We have to bring it out! As I mentioned earlier, there is new life within you that is longing to get out into the world around you. God works this life in us by virtue of the Holy Spirit, and we work it out of us by virtue of our obedience to His Word. Many times, when people hear the word *obedience*, they become discouraged. They think it implies following a bunch of rules and regulations that they probably could not keep anyway. However, Christians are wired to obey God. Obedience is not something that is difficult for a believer, in fact; it is in our very nature.

OUR INWARD LIFE IS GOD'S PRIORITY!

Jesus declared that it is what comes out of us that defiles us, not what goes into us (that is, physical things like food). First and foremost, God is extremely concerned about our hearts. He is also concerned about our external life, but He knows that lasting change will not occur on the outside unless there is change on the inside. In Matthew 12:35, what does Jesus mean by *"the good treasure of the heart"*? Our treasure is our value system. It is what we hold near and dear. As you already know, the heart (soul) is the seat of the mind, will, and emotions. It is the place where we make our decisions. It is the fountain of our passions, thoughts, desires, and affections.

In the original Greek, the idea conveyed in *"treasure"* is that of "the place in which good and precious things are collected and laid up," such as a coffer, treasury, storehouse, or repository. Every sin (a product of *"evil treasure"*) or righteous deed (a product of *"good treasure"*) comes from our heart. Before we ever do something wrong or right, the desire is stored in the repository of our heart. Since the heart is such a crucial place in relation to our spiritual lives, it is only fitting that real transformation begin there.

Remember, we first need to be born again, but after that, we must begin to change what is in our heart. How do we accomplish this task? Simple! Our thought life is the gateway to our heart. Everything that is carried out externally begins in our mind. Let me reiterate what Paul says in Romans 12:2: *"And be not conformed to this world: but be you transformed by the renewing of your mind, that you may prove what is that good, and acceptable, and perfect, will of God."*

In order to demonstrate the good, acceptable, and perfect will of God, we must have already renewed our minds. In other chapters, we've talked about the necessity of this transformation, but let's look more closely at what it means to renew our minds. The Greek word for *"renewing"* is *anakainosis*, which means "a renewal, renovation, complete change for the better." We have to renovate our thinking in order to experience a complete change for the better, which will produce lasting transformation in every area of our lives, including our ability to walk in the supernatural.

This concept seems simple enough, right? Yet, too often, we place very little emphasis on changing our thought life. Maybe we don't believe that the effects of renewing our mind are as powerful as the Bible claims they are. The fact remains that mind renewal is the only way to truly experience the fullness of what God has promised us in His Word. It is what gives our new nature its full potency. This is how we work out our salvation as we walk in the Spirit.

> BEFORE WE EVER DO SOMETHING WRONG OR RIGHT, THE DESIRE IS STORED IN THE REPOSITORY OF OUR HEART.

GOD'S RENOVATION PROJECT

In the subdivision where my wife and I live, we are seeing a plethora of new construction projects. It amazes me how fast houses are built these days. When I began to watch the construction workers build these new dwellings, it caused me to think about the internal renovation project of the Christian life. Our lives must be built and renovated according to the pattern of the living Word of God, the Lord Jesus Christ. Before we were saved, due to our fallen nature, we were involved in sinful activities and a corrupt world system. We built infrastructures in our fleshy way of thinking that need to be torn down and replaced with kingdom infrastructures that glorify God and manifest His power and blessings in our lives. This is a spiritual renovation of our way of thinking that enables us to internalize God's truth.

Many people have painted the walls of their emotions the wrong color, and as a result, they are not getting the best out of their "home." They have living rooms of rejection and basements of depression that need to be refurbished. Paul says that the result of our mind renovation is transformation. This is a powerful thought that is derived from the Greek word *metamorphoo*, which means "to change into another form, to transform, to transfigure."

In Matthew 17:1–2, we read:

And after six days Jesus takes Peter, James, and John his brother, and brings them up into a high mountain apart, and was transfigured before them: and His face did shine as the sun, and His raiment was white as the light.

The Greek word for *"transfigured"* in this passage is the same word used in Romans 12:2 for *"transformed."* Jesus took on another form. His faced shined like the sun and His clothing became as white as light. I believe this glorified appearance was Jesus's true form. He did not suddenly become something different from His nature. He simply allowed His true nature to shine! Note that Jesus did not experience this transfiguration by Himself. In my opinion, He invited His disciples to see Him in that state so that they would begin to see themselves the way God intended them to.

Similarly, as we renew our minds with God's Word, the glory and splendor that He has placed within us will be demonstrated externally. That with which God has impregnated our spirits will begin to work its way out of us for ourselves and others to see. The Lord has called us to manifest to the world what a child of God really looks like. We are to allow the light of the Holy Spirit to shine through us and thereby pierce the darkness so that people around us will never be the same again. When others are allowed to see the splendor that is inside of us, they will want more of God's manifest presence in their own lives.

God has called us to be His personal renovation projects! When our minds are renovated, our lives will be transformed, demonstrating the will of God. What is God's will? His will is for people everywhere to be transformed into the image of His Son Jesus Christ. Those who work in the field of building renovation gain referrals based on the quality of their work. What do your words and actions demonstrate about your life? Do people want to find out who your Renovator is?

WHAT PROGRESS ARE YOU MAKING ON RENEWING YOUR MIND ACCORDING TO GOD'S WILL? HOW CAN YOU FURTHER THAT PROGRESS?

WHAT ABOUT REPENTANCE?

We all know that repentance is a very important part of the kingdom message. There are many pastors and other church leaders who would argue that there is not enough preaching about repentance in the church today. "We should preach more against sin and rebellion against God and tell people how wrong they are!" they say. I agree that the church needs to preach repentance, but what does repentance really mean from God's perspective? While those of us in ministry are very well acquainted with the importance of repentance, have we presented this idea the way the Scriptures do?

On the day of Pentecost, Peter said to the people, *"Repent, and be baptized every one of you in the name of Jesus Christ for the remission of sins, and you shall receive the gift of the Holy Ghost"* (Acts 2:38). What repentance was Peter talking about? Is it simply a religious exercise of the will? The Greek word for *"repent"* is *metanoeo*, and it means "to change one's mind." When sinners come to repentance, it means that they have changed their mind about God, about themselves, and about their sin, recognizing their need for Christ. Why is this concept so vital—not only for new Christians but also for all believers? Because, as we have seen, in order to be filled with the Holy Spirit and live out the Christian life, we have to change the way we think. The reason why we are seeing so little repentance in the church today is because very few people understand what it really means. Repentance means undergoing a radical shift in our thinking about every aspect of our lives.

THE MYSTERY OF TRUE REPENTANCE

To further explore this concept, let's read what Jesus said in Luke 5:32–39:

I came not to call the righteous, but sinners to repentance. And they said to Him, Why do the disciples of John fast often, and make prayers, and likewise the disciples of the Pharisees; but yours eat and drink? And He said to them, Can you make the children of the bridechamber fast, while the bridegroom is with them? But the days will come, when the bridegroom shall be taken away from them, and then shall they fast in those days. And He spoke also a parable to them; No man puts a piece of a new garment upon an old; if otherwise, then both the new makes a rent, and the piece that was taken out of the new agrees not with the old. And no man puts new wine into old bottles; else the new wine will burst the bottles, and be spilled, and the bottles shall perish. But new wine must be put into new bottles; and both are preserved. No man also having drunk old wine immediately desires new: for he says, The old is better.

In this passage, Jesus, our Master Teacher, eloquently explains the concept of true repentance. Our Lord compares His ministry of calling sinners to repentance to the process of putting wine into bottles. According to Jesus, to place new wine in an old bottle would actually cause the bottle to burst. Remember that the context of this parable is repentance. When you attempt to get an unrepentant person to embrace the kingdom life, it is like trying to put new wine in an old bottle—they would be unable to contain it.

The "bottles" mentioned in this parable were actually leather bags called wineskins. Old wineskins were not able to hold newly fermented wine due to the chemical composition of the wine and the wear and tear in the leather. In order to accommodate new wine, the skin had to be new from the inside out. Jesus is talking about people changing the way they think, being made new on the inside. Before they could embrace a spiritual kingdom, they had to have a paradigm shift.

This is the essence of true repentance. Before people can live the way God has called them to live, they must think differently about the state of their life and to whom their life belongs. As a leader, it is part of my ministry assignment to call people to genuine repentance. This is not a call to pseudo-religious piety; it is a challenge to change their whole mindset. When we challenge people to think differently, they will be in a position to embrace kingdom life. This change in thinking will result in a radical change of their lifestyle.

A COMPLETE PARADIGM SHIFT

It is not enough to change the order of our church services or the way we dress; we must have a complete paradigm shift in church culture as we know it. This is the essential truth we have been discussing throughout this book—we have to shift from an old-covenant, performance-based attitude to a new-covenant, grace-empowered outlook. We must understand that repentance is not merely about behavioral adjustments but about radical inner transformation. Such an understanding marks the difference between churches filled with carnal Christians and churches filled with grace-empowered believers in Jesus who have so much of God's life inside of them that it overflows to change the cultures of communities, cities, and nations.

When our thinking changes, our lives will change. Once we embrace true repentance according to God's Word, we will be able to turn away from our sin and walk in righteousness and true holiness. We will do as Jesus commanded the woman caught in adultery—we will go and sin no more! (See John 8:1–11.) And as we renew our minds, we will be able to fulfill the Great Commission, bringing many to Christ as we do miracles, signs, and wonders in His name!

WHEN PEOPLE ARE ALLOWED TO SEE THE SPLENDOR INSIDE OF YOU, THEY WILL WANT MORE OF GOD'S MANIFEST PRESENCE IN THEIR OWN LIVES.

VICTORY PRAYER

Father, in the name of Your Son Jesus Christ, I thank You that my inward life is Your priority. I praise You that You change me from the inside out. You are my holiness! I declare that Your Spirit is working within me to will and to do Your good pleasure. I work out my own salvation with fear and trembling. I decide to manifest what You have deposited within me. I repent from sin and from wrong ways of thinking. I declare that I think according to the

Word of God, not according to religion and tradition. Father, use my life as a supernatural renovation project that draws people into Your kingdom and brings You glory. In Jesus's name, amen!

UNLOCKING THE CODE OF THE SUPERNATURAL INSIGHTS

1. What does it mean for us to "work out our salvation with fear and trembling"?

2. What is God's role in this process?

3. In Romans 12:2, what does the Greek word for *"renewing"* signify? How can we apply this concept to our lives?

4. What is the true meaning of repentance?

13

CHRIST-CONSCIOUSNESS

*"For I determined not to know any thing among you,
save Jesus Christ, and Him crucified."*
—1 Corinthians 2:2

In the early stages of my Christian life, I was taught that the goal of a believer was to stop sinning. Once I got the sin out of my life, God could really use me. This idea was reinforced through Sunday sermons in which the pastor emphasized to us in the congregation how angry and bitter we were, and how much we did not love God. As I absorbed this perspective, the most interesting thing started to happen—I became more angry and bitter! The more I tried to focus my energies on getting rid of sin, the more sin crept into my life. I was confused!

Every Sunday, I went to the altar to repent of the sins that I had committed the previous week. In a sense, church became a sort of "spiritual car wash" for me. I went in expecting to be convicted of my sin, feel bad, and ultimately tell God I was sorry. This went on for years as a pattern of ups and downs became more prevalent in my everyday life as a believer. I certainly was not living in victory. As I observed the people around me, I noticed that they, too, were going through the same cycle.

What were we missing? The truth is, we were being taught sin-consciousness. Sin-consciousness is a frame of mind in which we invest most of our spiritual and mental energy on our sinful state, our failures, and our frailties rather than on our position of righteousness in Christ. It is a state in which we continually think about how much we have done wrong and how horrible our mistakes have been. This approach is highly performance-oriented and, as you might imagine, tremendously harmful to a believer's spiritual health and effectiveness.

GODLY AFFIRMATION

I have a daughter named Ella. Because she is young, she is in the beginning stages of her personal development. She is bashful at times and frequently makes mistakes. Imagine how it would be if, every time she did something wrong, I spent two weeks telling her how many mistakes she had made and how bad she was. Imagine if I always chastised her for her shortcomings and never affirmed her or told her how much I loved her. Such treatment could become emotionally abusive very quickly. Why? Children need affirmation. They require an environment in which a parent or other adult lovingly corrects their wrong behavior while constantly encouraging them and reminding them of their worth and value.

IS YOUR MINDSET USUALLY ONE OF SIN-CONSCIOUSNESS OR CHRIST-CONSCIOUSNESS? HOW CAN YOU BECOME MORE CHRIST-CONSCIOUS IN YOUR DAILY LIFE?

Dealing with a child solely on the basis of their faults is an imbalanced approach. Ella needs me, as her father, to regularly remind her of her place in my heart. She needs to be corrected in a healthy way that reaffirms positive behavior and discourages wrongdoing. It is important for my daughter to know who she is, to be continually conscious of her identity in God and as a cherished member of our family.

On the other hand, it would be equally problematic for me to disregard any wrong behavior my daughter displays based on a desire to maintain a friendship with her. This would be emotionally and spiritually damaging to her because I would not be providing her with healthy boundaries or teaching her to follow the ways of the Lord.

Similarly, we are God's spiritual children, and He knows that we need His love and affirmation for our spiritual and emotional health. He desires to demonstrate His deep love for us. And He also knows that, without the assurance of that love, we cannot become all that He has called us to be. Pastors must understand these truths because when leaders neglect to give believers godly affirmation according to the Word of God, it can lead to spiritual abuse.

> GOD DESIRES TO DEMONSTRATE HIS DEEP LOVE FOR US. HE KNOWS THAT, WITHOUT THE ASSURANCE OF HIS LOVE, WE CANNOT BECOME ALL THAT HE HAS CALLED US TO BE.

In those early years of my faith, the reason I became stuck in a pattern of defeat was that I was following a simple principle called "The Law of Manifestation." This law says that the things we continually set our mind on will ultimately manifest in our lives. The Bible explains it in this way: *"For as he thinks in his heart, so is he"* (Proverbs 23:7). The Law of Manifestation can produce positive or negative results, depending upon what we focus on. I was focusing my thoughts on my sin rather than on the finished work of Christ on my behalf. Consequently, I naturally manifested defeat instead of victory.

Paul told the Corinthian believers that he was determined not to "*know*" anything among them except Jesus Christ, and Him crucified. This is a profound truth! Why did Paul say this? He tells us in 1 Corinthians 2:5:

That your faith should not stand in the wisdom of men, but in the power of God.

Paul did not want the Corinthians to base their understanding of God on man's wisdom. He did not want them to be caught up in the vain philosophy of the world. Therefore, he determined not to teach them anything except Christ. This was the ethos of Paul's power as a preacher of the gospel and as a Christian in general. In 1 Corinthians 2:2, the Greek word translated "*know*" is *eido*, among whose meanings is "to discern" or "to pay attention." Paul was focused on Jesus Christ. The more Paul was conscious of Christ and His power, the more the power of Christ became available to him. This is what I refer to as Christ-consciousness, which is the antithesis of sin-consciousness. Sin-consciousness focuses on us, while Christ-consciousness focuses on Jesus. The more we are conscious of Christ and His finished work on the cross, the more we will walk in victory in every area of our lives. Through Jesus's death, burial, and resurrection, the power of sin has been destroyed in the lives of born-again believers.

WHAT ABOUT CONVICTION OF SIN?

Sometimes, the issue of "conviction of sin" can be a sensitive subject, especially because of the misrepresentation of grace that we have seen in the church in recent years. The purpose of this book is to empower believers who are genuinely seeking to walk in victory in their lives but have not been able to do so because of their bondage to guilt, shame, and condemnation. I have shared how I was bound in this way for many years and could not come out of that captivity until I discovered the mystery of the new-creation life.

Like many Christians, I had been taught that one of the evidentiary proofs of being a believer is conviction of one's sins. After all, we should feel bad when we do wrong; we can't just run around without thinking about our sins. Right? Absolutely! We should definitely cease from sinning, and we should be remorseful if and when we do commit sin. The question remains, what role does conviction of sin play in our lives as believers who have come into a saving relationship with Jesus?

I have heard countless Christians say, "The Spirit convicted me!" What most people mean by this is that they feel bad about something they did wrong. They are referring to their conscience bothering them. The problem is that erroneous teaching in the church has caused people to apply the term *conviction* to this sense of having done wrong. This faulty understanding has contributed to our problems with sin-consciousness.

THE SPIRIT CONVICTS THE WORLD OF SIN

As we begin to examine this issue more closely, I want to define the term *conviction* scripturally by exploring Jesus's statements in the following passage:

Nevertheless I tell you the truth; It is expedient for you that I go away: for if I go not away, the Comforter will not come to you; but if I depart, I will send Him to you. And when He is come, He will reprove the world of sin, and of righteousness, and of judgment: of sin, because they believe not on Me; of righteousness, because I go to My Father, and you see Me no more; of judgment, because the prince of this world is judged. —John 16:7–11

Here, Jesus outlines what will happen when He sends the Holy Spirit to His followers after His death, burial, resurrection, and ascension—and how the Spirit will work through believers as they preach the gospel to the world. According to this passage, there are three aspects to the Holy Spirit's assignment in the earth: He will *"reprove,"* or *"convict"* (NKJV), the world of (1) sin, (2) righteousness, and (3) judgment.

The Greek word rendered *"reprove"* is *elegcho*, among whose meanings is "to convict" or "to refute." With these particular meanings, there can be the sense of "a suggestion of shame of the person convicted" or "by conviction to bring to the light, to expose." The word can also mean "to reprehend severely," "to chide," "to admonish," and "to call to account." Now, I am a firm believer that we are to derive our revelation of God from His Word. That is why it is important to allow the context and content of this passage to interpret its meaning for us. If *"reprove"* or *"convict"* means to reprehend and to shame, then is Jesus saying that the Holy Spirit censures and shames believers every time they do something wrong? Absolutely not! Then, who is being addressed here, and what does the statement really mean?

John 16:9–11 highlights the purpose of each category in which the Holy Spirit convicts—sin, righteousness, and judgment. Jesus Christ has sent the Spirit to convict the *world* of its sin. Jesus specifically refers to the sin of unbelief here. Therefore, this reprehension, rebuke, and shame comes to the people of the world, not Christians. The Holy Spirit reproves people for sin because they have refused to believe in Jesus Christ. The Greek word translated *"world"* here is *kosmos*, which technically means the whole world. However, Jesus makes a distinction between two types of people in this passage by referring to *"you"* and *"they."* The Holy Spirit has a different role in dealing with each group.

HOW DID YOU EXPERIENCE THE HOLY SPIRIT'S

CONVICTION WHEN YOU FIRST CAME TO KNOW CHRIST?

The last time I checked, the church and the world were two different entities. Jesus said, *"If you were of the world, the world would love his own: but because you are not of the world, but I have chosen you out of the world, therefore the world hates you"* (John 15:19). Believers are not a part of the world system. So again, according to Scripture, the conviction of the sin of unbelief does not apply to believers but to unbelievers. Reproof, shame, guilt, and condemnation were never intended for those who are born again because we are no longer in unbelief regarding Christ. We can see that many people in the church have grossly misinterpreted this passage, taking it out of its original context. I know this may come as a shock to you, but the Holy Spirit does not, in this sense, convict born-again believers of their sins.

THE SPIRIT CONVINCES BELIEVERS OF THEIR RIGHTEOUSNESS

To be clear, every genuine believer must experience an initial conviction of sin. This is how we come to know our own dreadfulness as unregenerate sinners. When we were living according to the system of this world, it was the Holy Spirit who let us know that we were in unbelief. This was not a mental or emotional phenomenon; it was an inner spiritual revelation. When we heard the gospel for the first time, the Holy Spirit convicted us. He revealed to us our sinful state, showing us how filthy we were before a holy God. He told us that we had been living in unbelief and called us to account for our sin. When we confessed or admitted that we were, in fact, sinners in need of a Savior, believed in Jesus's sacrifice on the cross for us, and received Him into our lives, we were saved.

Thus, the first category of conviction that Jesus speaks about in John 16 applies to the unsaved. The second category applies to born-again believers. In verse 10, Jesus says, *"…of righteousness, because I go to My Father, and you see Me no more."* What does this statement indicate? The word for *"righteousness"* is *dikaiosune*, which means, in a broad sense, "the state of him who is as he ought to be," "righteousness," and "the condition acceptable to God." Even though Jesus uses this statement in conjunction with the world, we know, based on the harmony of Scripture, that the Holy Spirit cannot convince sinners of their righteousness. And Jesus's disciples were the ones who would "see Him no more." So, again, this aspect of conviction refers to the believer (living in the world).

This, my friend, is the true conviction of the Holy Spirit in the lives of believers—not of sin, but of righteousness. Once we are born again, the Spirit convicts, or convinces, us of our righteousness in Jesus. The Holy Spirit stands with us and makes us conscious of the living Christ. The word for *"righteousness"* in John 16:10 refers to "right standing" with God. So, we see that the Spirit brings to light, persuades us of, and affirms our position of righteousness in Christ. This form of conviction is totally different from what people in the world experience when they are convicted of their unbelief.

THE TRUE CONVICTION OF THE HOLY SPIRIT IN THE LIVES OF BELIEVERS IS NOT OF SIN BUT OF RIGHTEOUSNESS.

THE SPIRIT CONVINCES US THAT SATAN HAS BEEN JUDGED

In John 16:11, Jesus speaks of the third category: *"…of judgment, because the prince of this world is judged."* The Holy Spirit convinces us of the fact that *"the prince of this world,"* Satan, has been judged by God. The Spirit has issued a sentence of judgment and destruction on Satan to the world on behalf of believers.

DIFFERENT DIMENSIONS OF CONVICTION

A good analogy of the effects of the Holy Spirit's conviction on people is the body of laws in a country, issued for people's safety and welfare. The laws apply to everyone in the nation, and these laws bring either benefits or penalties, depending on how people respond to them. For the lawbreakers, the laws are against them and stand as an indictment of their transgressions. For the law keepers, the laws stand as a confirmation of the protection of their rights and privileges provided under those ordinances.

Thus, the Holy Spirit convicts the entire world, but people in the world (cosmos) experience a different dimension of conviction depending on which side of the "law" they stand on. We who are in Christ stand in belief of the truth, and therefore the Holy Spirit confirms for us our position of righteousness.

Note again that nothing is mentioned in this passage about the Spirit telling a believer how bad they are. We are not meant to walk around with sin-consciousness but Christ-consciousness. The Holy Spirit convinces us of our righteousness in Christ and of our victory over the enemy.

CONVICTION VERSUS CONTRITION

At this point, we need to address the subject of conviction versus contrition because many people in the body of Christ are being oppressed by the enemy in this area of their lives. It will be helpful for us to review the truths in the following passage from 2 Corinthians:

For though I [Paul] made you sorry with a letter, I do not repent, though I did repent: for I perceive that the same epistle has made you sorry, though it were but for a season. Now I rejoice, not that you were made sorry, but that you sorrowed to repentance: for you were made sorry after a godly manner, that you might receive damage by us in nothing. For godly sorrow works repentance to salvation not to be repented of: but the sorrow of the world works death. For behold this selfsame thing, that you sorrowed after a godly sort, what carefulness it wrought in you, yea, what clearing of yourselves, yea, what indignation, yea, what fear, yea, what vehement desire, yea, what zeal, yea, what revenge ["vindication" NKJV]! In all things you have approved yourselves to be clear in this matter.

—2 Corinthians 7:8–11

As a pastor, I have seen countless people come down to the altar after a service, in the name of "conviction of sin," who weep and mourn on their knees over their wrongdoings but then go right back to their sinful lifestyles after they leave the church. I asked the Lord, "What is the problem? Why are so many people still bound after hearing the unadulterated Word of God?" God began to show me that the people were not genuinely repenting; they were simply responding emotionally to their guilt and shame.

Such a response was never initiated by the Holy Spirit! Responding in this way is not unique to Christians. Many sinners who do wrong are convinced that they have transgressed, and they feel guilty for it, but this feeling does not necessarily cause them to change.

How are we supposed to respond to obvious sin in our lives and ultimately change for the better? There is only one way: through *contrition.* The apostle Paul dealt with this very issue in the church at Corinth. Unfortunately, the Corinthians were well acquainted with sin. As a matter of fact, they had a huge problem with fornication. Culturally speaking, this church was chiefly made up of Greeks, and fornication was a huge part of ancient Greek culture. In fact, many of their idols were venerated through sexual immorality. Some of the newly converted Christians brought these carnal ideas into the church. Paul had addressed the issue of fornication in his first epistle to the Corinthians, specifically in regard to a situation in which a man in the church was having intercourse with his father's wife. (See 1 Corinthians 5.) He had instructed this young assembly of believers to put the fornicator out of the church for the purpose of removing this corrupting influence, which would hopefully also lead the man to repent. In 2 Corinthians, Paul congratulates the church for coming to a place of repentance. How did they arrive at that place?

GODLY SORROW

Paul attributes the church's ability to repent to something he calls *"godly sorrow"*: *"For godly sorrow works repentance to salvation not to be repented of: but the sorrow of the world works death"* (2 Corinthians 7:10). This is the type of sorrow the Holy Spirit produces within a believer. Again, the Holy Spirit is interested in manifesting the life of God inside of us, and when something impedes this life from flowing in and through us, He brings that area to our attention. He produces a godly contrition within us that motivates us to obey God in the areas in which we have previously disobeyed Him. In contrast, the sorrow of the world produces death (that is, separation from God). This sorrow is based on condemnation and guilt but results in no inner change. The sorrow that the Holy Spirit produces is based on the truth of God's Word and yields inner transformation.

Every genuine believer experiences godly sorrow, which is characterized by a love for God and a hatred of sin. This type of sorrow comes naturally to those who are born again. The distinction between worldly sorrow and godly sorrow is highlighted further in 2 Corinthians 7:11:

For behold this selfsame thing, that you sorrowed after a godly sort, what carefulness it wrought in you, yea, what clearing of yourselves, yea, what indignation, yea, what fear, yea, what vehement desire, yea, what zeal, yea, what revenge ["vindication" NKJV]! In all things you have approved yourselves to be clear in this matter.

The Word of God says that the Corinthians' godly sorrow produced a *"clearing"* of themselves. The Greek term for *"clearing"* is *apologia*, which means "a verbal defense" or "a speech in defense." The Holy Spirit defends our position as children of God by producing in our hearts a sorrow and remorse for sin. As with the believers in the Corinthian church, this sorrow and remorse demonstrates that we do not approve of our sin. Such a demonstration is a good sign that the Holy Spirit is at work in our lives and that we are, in fact, born again.

VICTORY PRAYER

Heavenly Father, I thank You for who You are and all that You have done for me. Help me to continually be Christ-conscious, rather than sin-conscious, so that I can walk in victory in every area of my life! Thank You that the Holy Spirit ministers to me to convince me of my righteousness in Jesus and to assure me that Satan has already been defeated. And thank You that, if I sin, Your grace produces godly sorrow within me so that I can immediately repent and experience inner transformation, having more and more love for You. In Jesus's name, amen!

UNLOCKING THE CODE OF THE SUPERNATURAL INSIGHTS

1. What is the "Law of Manifestation"? How can it bring either positive or negative results?

2. What are the three categories in which the Holy Spirit convicts?

3. Which of these categories apply to the world, and which apply to believers?

4. How does conviction in the life of an unsaved person differ from conviction in the life of a believer?

14

THE MINISTRY OF THE HOLY SPIRIT

"However when He, the Spirit of truth, is come,
He will guide you into all truth: for He shall not speak of Himself; but
whatsoever He shall hear, that shall He speak: and He will show you
things to come. He shall glorify Me: for He shall receive of Mine, and
shall show it to you."
—John 16:13–14

To receive the full ministry of the Holy Spirit in our lives, we must recognize who He is. Some cults and false religions teach that He is essentially a type of "force," but we know based on Scripture that the Holy Spirit is not a force—He is a Person. We must also keep in mind some foundational facts about Him.

First, the Holy Spirit is God, the third person of the Trinity. He was present at the beginning of creation, "[moving] *upon the face of the waters*" (Genesis 1:2). Second, He anointed Jesus and gave Him the supernatural power to carry out His earthly ministry. Third, He raised Jesus from the dead. Fourth, He is the regenerative Agent in salvation who quickens our dead human spirits, making us alive in Christ and joining us as one spirit with the Lord. Fifth, He possesses divine power, and He releases that power in our lives as we yield to Him. These are some serious attributes!

OUR COMFORTER AND ADVOCATE

The Holy Spirit is *the* most important Person in our lives because He is the One who reveals Jesus Christ to us and glorifies the Father. In John 16:7, Jesus declares that He will send us the Spirit as our *"Comforter."* This is good news! The Greek word for *"Comforter"* is *parakletos*, and it implies that one of the Spirit's functions is that of Helper or "legal assistant."

When is the last time you saw a lawyer turn against a client in the middle of a court preceding? This doesn't happen because the lawyer enters into an agreement to stand by and defend their client. Well, the Holy Spirit is our Advocate. As we saw in the previous chapter, His ministry in the life of born-again believers is not to condemn us for our sin but to comfort us in the truth of our righteousness in Christ.

HOW VICTORY COMES

It is important for us to understand how God brings about victory in our lives. Real conviction by the Holy Spirit is not superficial guilt that ultimately lands us in the same place we were in before. Real conviction reminds us of the holiness of God and produces reverential fear in our hearts. Real conviction is rooted in Christ-consciousness. The Holy Spirit points us to Christ as our Redeemer and Source.

Let's look again at John 16:13–14:

However when He, the Spirit of truth, is come, He will guide you into all truth: for He shall not speak of Himself; but whatsoever He shall hear, that shall He speak: and He will show you things to come. He shall glorify Me: for He shall receive of Mine, and shall show it to you.

The Holy Spirit has been assigned to guide us into all truth. He has been sent on a specific mission to glorify the Father in our lives. If you are born again, the Holy Spirit will not tell you how wicked you are because that is not His assignment. Nevertheless, make no mistake, the Spirit disciplines and directs us to bring us correction. He points out everything in our lives that does not line up with the truth of God's Word. New-creation believers must be convinced of the truth of God's Word, which is our source of faith and repentance.

We need to realize that we have a seed of righteousness within us that prevents us from continuing in willful sin. We have been born again of incorruptible seed. (See 1 Peter 1:23.) Again, this is an ontological reality that we need to bear out in our lives. Let me reiterate the warning that if you are looking for an excuse to continue in a sinful lifestyle, you are probably not born again. You must seriously consider your position before God, repent with godly sorrow, and receive Christ.

For example, if a Christian has bitterness in their heart that is keeping them from walking in the love of God toward another believer, the Holy Spirit will shine the light of God's Word on that issue, giving the Christian the truth they need to align their life accordingly. The Bible says, *"For whom the Lord loves He chastens, and scourges every son whom He receives"* (Hebrews 12:6). The Greek word for *"chastens"* in this verse is *paideuo*, among whose meanings is "to train children." It can refer to "those who are molding the character of others by reproof and admonition."

IN WHAT WAYS IS THE HOLY SPIRIT TEACHING YOU AND MOLDING YOUR CHARACTER?

The Holy Spirit is profoundly occupied with leading us to a place of victorious living. God is not interested in condemning you; He is too busy trying to manifest all that He is on the inside of you! Thus, a true believer does not take any joy in sinning against God; they will feel uncomfortable with sin because it goes against their true nature. The believer reverences God's presence in their life and does everything in their power to protect that presence.

Thus, the Holy Spirit corrects us, instructs us, and develops our character by reminding us and revealing to us what Jesus says. The Spirit directs us to God's truth concerning sin in our lives and shows us how to walk in the light. He has been given to the church to empower us to bring glory to God. If we would only take hold of these truths, we would never be the same.

GOD IS NOT INTERESTED IN CONDEMNING YOU; HE IS TOO BUSY TRYING TO MANIFEST ALL THAT HE IS ON THE INSIDE OF YOU!

THE SPIRIT OF ADOPTION

For you have not received the spirit of bondage again to fear; but you have received the Spirit of adoption, whereby we cry, Abba, Father.
—Romans 8:15

The Scriptures plainly tell us that we have not been given a spirit of bondage or slavery to fear. The Greek word translated "*fear*" is *phobos*, which can mean "dread" or "terror." It is the term from which we derive the English word *phobia*. A phobia is simply a chronic and unreasonable fear that distorts reality. When we are operating in fear, we cannot trust God or see Him the way He really is.

Many believers live in a state of constant terror. They are afraid that God does not love them, and if they make one false move, He will strike them down. This spirit of fear provokes them to live a superficial, performance-based

Christian life. Such a spirit does not come from God but from the enemy. Instead, as believers, we have received *"the Spirit of adoption."*

The Greek word for *"adoption"* is *huiothesia*, which indicates that we have been given a unique relationship with God as His sons and daughters. The Holy Spirit has sealed our adoption. (See Ephesians 1:13.) Our relationship with God is one of favor and preference. We are not spiritual stepchildren! We have the full rights and privileges of one who was actually born into the family. The Holy Spirit operates within us and causes our spirits to cry, *"Abba, Father."* *Abba* simply means "Daddy." Our spirits identify with God as our Father. We always desire to please Him because we are truly His children. The Bible further says:

The Spirit Itself bears witness with our spirit, that we are the children of God: and if children, then heirs; heirs of God, and joint-heirs with Christ; if so be that we suffer with Him, that we may be also glorified together. —Romans 8:16–17

The Holy Spirit *"bears witness with our spirit."* When the Scripture talks about the Holy Spirit "bearing witness," it is dealing with a concept called "joint witness." This means that our spirits and the Holy Spirit both testify that we are God's children. The Spirit is constantly reaffirming the truth that we are heirs of God and joint-heirs with Christ.

Remember, if you are truly born again, committing sin will always deeply disturb you. If you are a joint-heir with Christ, you can't go around sinning without feeling remorse. Your spirit no longer identifies with the world system. It goes against the grain. One day, I was watching television and something inappropriate came on the screen. Immediately, the Holy Spirit within me said, "No." I quickly turned away from the scene. The Holy Spirit was bearing joint witness with me that the sinful act being displayed on television did not line up with who He is or who I am—God's son! I never want to willfully sin against my heavenly Father. When I do commit sin, I am genuinely remorseful for my wrong, and through His power, I turn from that sin.

As we previously discussed, the Spirit does not shame or indict us concerning our sin. Those terms imply judicial guilt and condemnation.

Experiencing His correction is not the same as experiencing the conviction of unbelief as an unsaved person. Feelings of guilt and condemnation for sin are not from God. The reason we know such feelings are not from the Lord is because they do not bring Him glory. Again, the Holy Spirit's mission is to lead us into truth and bring glory to Jesus.

 WE HAVE BEEN GIVEN A UNIQUE RELATIONSHIP WITH GOD AS HIS SONS AND DAUGHTERS—A RELATIONSHIP OF FAVOR AND PREFERENCE.

SEALED FOR THE DAY OF REDEMPTION

And grieve not the Holy Spirit of God, whereby you are sealed to the day of redemption.   —Ephesians 4:30

The Greek word for *"grieve"* in this verse is *lupeo,* among whose meanings are "to make sorrowful," "to cause grief," and "to make one uneasy, cause him a scruple." When we violate the Word of God in any area of our lives, the Holy Spirit is made sorrowful and uneasy. This, in turn, makes us sorrowful, uneasy, and grieved inside. We must remember that, as a Person, the Holy Spirit has feelings and emotions. He completely disapproves of sin in our lives and therefore allows us to experience the same disapproval. It is similar to the relationship of unity between a loving husband and wife. If the husband or wife is upset, their spouse shares those emotions, whether of anger, frustration, hurt, or another feeling.

Therefore, the Holy Spirit leads us into truth and brings glory to God through our lives. He will always remind us of our true identity, which is one of *"righteousness and true holiness"* (Ephesians 4:24). If we have submitted to the lordship of Jesus Christ, we have been forgiven of our sins, and we are no longer under God's judgment. As new creations in Christ, we are filled with the same Spirit that raised Jesus from the dead. We are sons and daughters of God who walk in righteousness and are led by the Spirit!

VICTORY PRAYER

Father, I thank You for who You are and all that You have done for me. Thank You for revealing to me the nature of your precious Holy Spirit. Thank You, Holy Spirit, for leading me into all truth, which will transform my life. Thank You for being my Comforter and Guide. Lord Jesus Christ, I recognize that You are my Redeemer and Source. Through Your Spirit, I am convinced of my position of righteousness in You, and this revelation gives me the power to overcome sin in my life. Right now, I embrace the Spirit of Adoption. In Jesus's name, amen!

UNLOCKING THE CODE OF THE SUPERNATURAL INSIGHTS

1. What do believers have within them that prevents them from continuing in willful sin?

2. What is the Holy Spirit's mission in our lives?

3. What does it mean that we have received *the Spirit of adoption*?

4. In what way does the Holy Spirit "bear witness with our spirit"?

15

THE SPIRIT-FILLED LIFE

"And be not drunk with wine, wherein is excess;
but be filled with the Spirit."
—Ephesians 5:18

The Scriptures tell us that God has called His church to be filled with the Spirit. This is a foundational truth that many Christians still have not fully embraced—or have yet to experience. What does it mean to be filled with the Spirit, and what does the Spirit-filled life look like? I am glad you asked! Being filled with God's Spirit has several aspects, which we will explore in this chapter.

BE FILLED WITH THE HOLY SPIRIT

In Ephesians 5:18, the phrase *"be filled"* comes from the Greek word *pleroo*, among whose meanings are "to make full," "to supply liberally," and "to fill to the brim." Note that this verb is expressed in the imperative mood. It is a command. God commands us to be filled to the brim with His Holy Spirit!

Being filled with the Spirit is not optional. And it is not a one-time event—it is a continual filling. This is not just a religious experience. It means to actively yield the control of our lives to the Holy Spirit. God wants us to be ruled by His Spirit. I believe that we should submit to the Spirit more and more every day so that His nature and power can fill us to the brim. When we do this, we will no longer be carnal but spiritual. We will no longer be lustful but loving. We will no longer be judgmental but merciful. The more we are filled with the Holy Spirit, the more the Spirit's influence will saturate every area of our lives. This point is so vital that it cannot be overstated. The only life for the Christian is the Spirit-filled life!

BE BAPTIZED IN THE HOLY SPIRIT

In the book of Acts, we see another type of filling—the baptism in the Holy Spirit. I believe that receiving this baptism is necessary for the infilling we are commanded to experience in Ephesians 5.

And when the day of Pentecost was fully come, they were all with one accord in one place. And suddenly there came a sound from heaven as of a rushing mighty wind, and it filled all the house where they were sitting. And there appeared to them cloven tongues like as of fire, and it sat upon each of them. And they were all filled with the Holy Ghost, and began to speak with other tongues, as the Spirit gave them utterance.   —Acts 2:1–4

ARE YOU BEING CONTINUALLY FILLED WITH THE SPIRIT?

The outpouring of the Holy Spirit at Pentecost was a momentous event for the New Testament church. In fact, this occasion was so important to Jesus that He had instructed His disciples not to leave Jerusalem until they had received *"the promise of the Father"*:

> *And, being assembled together with them, commanded them that they should not depart from Jerusalem, but wait for the promise of the Father, which, says He, you have heard of Me. For John truly baptized with water; but you shall be baptized with the Holy Ghost not many days from now.*   —Acts 1:4–5

The Father had promised the coming of the Spirit, and Jesus told His disciples to expect it. Jesus did not refer to this supernatural manifestation as *a* promise, but as *the* promise. This was the big one. This was the promise that Jesus had spoken about throughout the three and a half years of His earthly ministry.

What, specifically, was this promise? Jesus explained it in Acts 1:8:

> *But you shall receive power, after that the Holy Ghost is come upon you: and you shall be witnesses to Me both in Jerusalem, and in all Judaea, and in Samaria, and to the uttermost part of the earth.*

Jesus said that once the disciples received the baptism in the Holy Spirit, they would have power to be witnesses for Him. This power was unlike anything they had ever seen or experienced prior to His ascension. The Greek word for *"power"* here is *dynamis*, which we defined earlier as "explosive power." Another meaning is "inherent power; power residing in a thing by virtue of its nature, or which a person or thing exerts and puts forth."

AUTHORITY

Earlier in His ministry, Jesus had told His disciples, *"Behold, I give to you power to tread on serpents and scorpions, and over all the power of the enemy: and nothing shall by any means hurt you"* (Luke 10:19). Our Lord made this statement prior to His death, resurrection, and ascension. The question is, if Jesus had already given His disciples power, why did they need more?

The Greek word for *"power"* in this verse is not *dynamis* but *exousia*, which means "authority." The disciples already had spiritual authority by virtue of their relationship with Jesus. He had delegated this authority to them. But they needed *power* in order to be His witnesses. What is the difference? Authority is an external endowment, whereas power is an internal capacity.

To give an illustration of this point, the main reason for police officers to wear badges is so that people can recognize the officers' legal authority. If you were driving your car, and a law enforcement officer pulled you over, you would not yield to them until you saw their badge, which represents their authority. The disciples needed authority in order to exercise kingdom government in the world, including ruling over demonic spirits. And every believer in Jesus has the right and authority to defeat the enemy, casting out demons in Jesus's name.

AUTHORITY IS AN EXTERNAL ENDOWMENT, WHEREAS POWER IS AN INTERNAL CAPACITY.

POWER

As I mentioned above, *dynamis* power is an altogether different endowment than *exousia* power because it is internal. It is the power to exercise one's authority. It is the gift of the divine ability to execute or manifest something. Let's return to the analogy of law enforcement officers. If police officers are off duty, they still retain their inherent abilities even though they are not wearing their badges. Their instincts, their ability to react quickly to situations, and their desire to protect people stay with them twenty-four hours a day because these are inner qualities. Officers also carry guns to enforce their authority, and if they ever need to use their guns off duty, they will employ the same skill with them that they would if they were on duty wearing their badges. This inherent ability is the type of power Jesus was referring to in the book of Acts. And it can only come through receiving the baptism in the Holy Spirit.

SUBMERGED IN THE HOLY SPIRIT

For John truly baptized with water; but you shall be baptized with the Holy Ghost not many days from now.   —Acts 1:5

The Greek word for *"baptized"* is *baptizo*, which means "to immerse" or "to submerge." In this verse, Jesus was telling His disciples that, after He left, they would be submerged in the fire of the Holy Spirit. And that is what took place on the day of Pentecost. The followers of Jesus were all *"filled with the Holy Ghost,"* with the initial evidence of speaking in other tongues, *"as the Spirit gave them utterance."* (See Acts 2:4.) (The Greek word for *"filled"* here is *pimplemi*, which simply means "to be filled.")

HOW HAS YOUR LIFE CHANGED SINCE YOU RECEIVED THE BAPTISM IN THE HOLY SPIRIT?

When the disciples were baptized in the Spirit, they were given the ability to speak with other tongues. I understand that speaking in tongues can be a controversial topic, but I believe God continues to give this gift and that it is absolutely necessary to enable the church to walk in supernatural power. I am an old-fashioned guy—if the Bible says it, I just believe it. It is really sad that some so-called educated Christian leaders deny the scriptural gift of the baptism in the Holy Spirit. No wonder there are so many churches today in which the members exhibit carnality and defeat. Whole denominations have rejected a significant aspect of the ministry of the most important Person on earth. Yet every born-again believer has the blood-bought right to be Spirit-filled and to speak in other tongues as the Holy Spirit enables them.

On the day of Pentecost, the early disciples received spiritual empowerment with the gift of tongues, enabling them to proclaim the message of God's kingdom with boldness, purity, and conviction. In Acts 2:6–11, we see that as the disciples began to speak in other tongues, supernatural power was released into the atmosphere. This power drew people who had gathered in Jerusalem from many nations to celebrate Pentecost. In their own native languages, they heard about *the wonderful works of God*" (verse 11). What an amazing demonstration of God's power!

In the book of Joel, God promised that He would pour out His Spirit on all flesh. (See Joel 2:28–29.) The day of Pentecost marked the manifestation of that promise through the early church. By the end of the apostle Peter's sermon following this outpouring, the people listening were so supernaturally convicted that three thousand souls were added to the church in one day. Now, that's an altar call! What was the secret weapon? The baptism in the Holy Spirit. Every believer must experience Holy Spirit baptism to live a life of victory and serve God with power.

SO MUCH MORE!

It is important to keep in mind that the purpose of the baptism in the Holy Spirit is not just to enable us to speak in tongues for its own sake. We must pray in tongues in order to speak forth mysteries in the spirit realm. But again, speaking in tongues is not the main evidence or purpose of being filled with the Holy Spirit, although it is often the *initial* evidence. Let's now look at several effects of the baptism.

First, the gift of public tongues is a sign to unbelievers. In 1 Corinthians 14:21–22, we read:

In the law it is written, With men of other tongues and other lips will I speak to this people; and yet for all that will they not hear Me, says the Lord. Wherefore tongues are for a sign, not to them that believe, but to them that believe not: but prophesying serves not for them that believe not, but for them which believe.

The Scriptures are clear about the importance of tongues. When we speak in tongues privately, we are spiritually strengthened and enabled to intercede for God's will to be done on earth as it is in heaven. And, as we just read, public tongues in an assembly of Christians is a sign to unbelievers about the reality of God's presence and power.

Second, the baptism in the Spirit serves to unify the church. The Holy Spirit is the only Person who can unite people—regardless of their different races, genders, nationalities, or ethnicities. He is the only One who can transcend all language barriers and cause the body of Christ to hear one heavenly sound. Oh, if only the church as a whole would return to its New-Testament roots! If the baptism in the Holy Spirit was necessary for the early church, it is necessary for us today.

Third, the main purpose of being filled with the Holy Spirit is so that we can be witnesses to Christ!

But you shall receive power, after that the Holy Ghost is come upon you: and you shall be witnesses to Me both in Jerusalem, and in all Judaea, and in Samaria, and to the uttermost part of the earth.

—Acts 1:8

The Greek word translated *"witnesses"* in this verse is *martys*, which can signify testifying in a legal sense. In a historical sense, the word can refer to "one who is a spectator of anything, e.g., of a contest." It speaks of someone who can bear witness to the truth of something. The English word *martyr* is derived from this term. The members of the early church were to bear witness to the resurrection of Jesus Christ by dying to themselves and testifying about the kingdom of God. How did they perform this task? By living a resurrected life. How were they able to live a resurrected life? By being filled with the Holy Spirit. It takes supernatural power to live this Christian life!

THE MYSTERY OF THE SPIRIT

Let me emphasize again that the supernatural power of the Holy Spirit is to be demonstrated in every area of our lives. When we are filled with the same Spirit who raised Jesus from the dead, our lives are full of victory. We no longer seek our own wills or agendas because we have been crucified with Christ to follow Him and live in His power.

Such a lifestyle is, in fact, the complete evidence of our being filled with the Holy Spirit. Through the years, I have observed people who speak in tongues but whose lives are full of defeat. How can we speak in tongues and claim that we are filled with the Holy Spirit when our hearts are full of hatred, bitterness, and rebellion against God? How can we say that we are filled with the Holy Spirit when our lives are not characterized by holiness? I believe that when such is the case in the life of a believer, it has to do with a wrong understanding of what it really means to live a Spirit-filled life.

> WHEN WE ARE FILLED WITH THE SAME
> SPIRIT WHO RAISED JESUS FROM THE DEAD,
> OUR LIVES ARE FULL OF VICTORY.

Make no mistake, I speak in tongues fluently and frequently. I believe that the gift of tongues is one of the most necessary and powerful weapons any believer can have in their arsenal. Yet our arsenal is to be coupled with a lifestyle that glorifies God. Speaking in tongues is just the beginning of the Spirit-filled life. It is not enough merely to speak in tongues. We must have an overflow of supernatural anointing that enables us to live the way Jesus lived when He walked the earth. Through this anointing, we are empowered to live above sin. We can deny our fleshly desires. We have the sovereign ability to forgive those who have wounded us and to love the unlovable. These victories are all evidence that we have been immersed in the Spirit of the living God.

When the third person of the Trinity is resident in our spirits, we have no reason to be defeated! We have heavenly power available to us at all times. Why should we be any less powerful than the believers in the early church were? As a matter of fact, I believe we should be even more powerful than they were! The early church did not have the completed New Testament to read, with all its revelation, examples, and instructions, to know exactly what to do. We have been given the explosive combination of the Spirit and the Word. This combination will release supernatural power for every believer.

Can you imagine how the church will look when we settle the issue of sin and the law, and then move on to perfection in the Spirit? Can you imagine the impact the body of Christ will have on the world when we are filled with the love and power of God?

 WE HAVE BEEN GIVEN THE EXPLOSIVE COMBINATION OF THE SPIRIT AND THE WORD. THIS COMBINATION WILL RELEASE SUPERNATURAL POWER FOR EVERY BELIEVER.

VICTORY PRAYER

Father, I honor You today and praise You for who You are. I recognize that the Holy Spirit is the most important Person on earth because He reveals Jesus Christ to us and brings glory to the Father and the Son. Today, I desire to be filled with the Holy Spirit with the evidence of speaking in other tongues as the Spirit gives me utterance. I also receive the evidence and fruit of victorious living. From this day forward, I declare that I am a witness to the resurrection of Jesus Christ because of the Spirit's power at work in me. I operate in supernatural authority and power to transform the atmosphere around me. Through the Holy Spirit, I am enabled to walk in love, speak the truth, testify to You, and overcome sin in every area of my life. In Jesus's name, amen!

UNLOCKING THE CODE OF THE SUPERNATURAL INSIGHTS

1. Is the command to be filled with the Holy Spirit optional? Why or why not?

2. List some meanings of the phrase *"be filled"* from the Greek word *pleroo* in Ephesians 5:18.

3. What are several purposes of the baptism in the Holy Spirit?

4. What "explosive combination" have we been given to release supernatural power in our lives?

MIRACLE TESTIMONY

HEALED OF RHEUMATOID ARTHRITIS

We must always remember that everything the Father has given us is on the basis of Jesus's sacrifice on the cross and triumphant resurrection. This means that God has blessed us for Jesus's sake. God has forgiven us for Jesus's sake. God has healed us for Jesus's sake. We have a responsibility to recognize this spiritual reality and live according to it. Many people don't enjoy the abundant life because they insist on being justified or rewarded for their own righteousness and, sometimes, for their own "rightness."

This reminds me of the testimony of a woman whose body had been ravaged by rheumatoid arthritis. She was in excruciating pain all the time, unable to move her fingers or enjoy normal motor function. One day, in a healing meeting, I began to pray for such conditions. As this woman came to the altar, the Lord told me to lead people in a prayer of release and forgiveness. It turns out that this woman had been through a very nasty divorce and, as a result, had allowed bitterness and unforgiveness to creep into her heart. Because she had refused to forgive, she had been unable to receive her healing. However, the moment she released her husband and forgave him, she was instantly healed! Hallelujah!

Why did this happen? The woman finally let go of her "right" to be angry. And by letting go of her own righteousness, she was freed to receive what God had already provided for her.

The same principle applies to us. The moment we let go of our own righteousness, we can receive Christ's righteousness. This is a major key in unlocking the code of the supernatural.

16

ONE NEW MAN

"But now in Christ Jesus you who sometimes were far off are made near by the blood of Christ. For He is our peace, who has made both one, and has broken down the middle wall of partition between us; having abolished in His flesh the enmity, even the law of commandments contained in ordinances; for to make in Himself of two one new man, so making peace."
—Ephesians 2:13–15

So far, we have examined what it means to be a new creation according to the Scriptures. We have talked about the fact that Christianity was never intended to be a religion but, rather, a living relationship with Jesus Christ. We have discussed the Spirit-filled life and the implications this life has on both individual Christians and the church at large. However, to fully understand the mystery and power of our new nature, we must also explore the *"one new man"* concept that Paul introduces in Ephesians 2.

BROUGHT NEAR TO GOD

I love the book of Ephesians because, although is one of the most difficult books in the Bible to understand, it is also one of the primary texts that unveil the mystery of our new nature. In Ephesians 2:13, Paul says that we *"who sometimes were far off are made near by the blood of Christ."* What does he mean by this statement? Paul is speaking as a Jew to Gentiles, and he is referring to God's special covenant with Israel.

Many Christians don't understand the concept of covenant. In fact, a number of Christians adhere to a concept called "Replacement Theology." This theological position asserts that God's covenant with Israel no longer applies because Israel has been replaced by the church. I am not going to go into much detail, but I will say that this is a very dangerous belief system introduced within the first few centuries of Christianity and accepted by Martin Luther and others of the Protestant Reformation. We must make sure that our belief systems are based, in their entirety, on the Word of God.

God chose Abraham to be the father of many nations. (See Genesis 17:4–5.) He revealed Himself to Abraham as Jehovah Jireh, the Provider (see Genesis 22:1–18) and made a covenant between Abraham and his descendants for *"a thousand generations"* (see Psalm 105:8–10).

God had called Abraham to come out of the land of Ur, which was a pagan nation. Abraham (Abram) was an idol worshipper when the Lord first spoke to him, but God changed his name and commissioned him to go and establish a new nation. This nation was composed of the Israelites, or the Jewish people. The phrase *"far off"* in Ephesians 2:13 comes from the Greek word *makran*, which means "far," or "a great way." The Gentiles were a great distance away from God because they were outside of His original covenant with Israel.

God's original plan was for His people to be a light, shining His glory to the nations of the earth and drawing them to Him. In fact, the Bible says that through Abraham (Israel), all the nations of the earth would be blessed. (See Genesis 18:18.) Thus, although the non-Jewish people groups of the earth were outside of the original covenant, God promised that through the descendants of Abraham, these people groups would share in the blessings.

From eternity past, God ordained that the Gentiles would come into covenant with Him—a covenant that has both spiritual and physical blessings attached to it. Paul says that the blood of Christ, the Messiah, was the bridge that brought the Gentiles into covenant relationship with God. We were spiritually brought near to God by Jesus's sacrifice.

The word *"near"* in this passage has greater implications than we may realize. It is translated from the Greek term *engys*, which means "near, of place and position" and can refer to "those who have near access to God." In other words, the blood of Jesus Christ has given the Gentiles access to the original covenant that God made with Israel—and much more. Through the blood of Jesus Christ, we are no longer *"aliens"*:

At that time you were without Christ, being aliens from the common-wealth of Israel, and strangers from the covenants of promise, having no hope, and without God in the world. —Ephesians 2:12

IN WHAT WAYS CAN YOU THANK GOD TODAY THAT YOU HAVE BEEN BROUGHT NEAR TO HIM IN CHRIST, RECEIVING FULL CITIZENSHIP IN HIS KINGDOM?

An alien is a foreigner who does not have political, social, or economic rights and benefits in the country in which they live. Just as someone who comes into the United States without a visa would be considered an illegal alien, so Gentiles do not have a legal right to the promises of God—apart from the blood of Jesus. Jesus's blood has given us citizenship!

CHRIST IS OUR PEACE!

Paul also says that Jesus Christ has become our peace. He did not say that Jesus has *given* us peace, but that *"He is our peace"* (Ephesians 2:14). The Greek word translated *"peace"* in this verse is *eirene*, which is a very strong term. Among its meanings are "a state of national tranquility," including the sense of "exemption from the rage and havoc of war"; "security, safety, prosperity, felicity (because peace and harmony make and keep things safe and prosperous)"; and "peace between individuals, i.e., harmony, concord." Thus, Jesus Christ has become our Source of tranquility, security, safety, prosperity, and freedom from rage and turmoil. We are stabilized, empowered, secured, and blessed because of Jesus.

Throughout the Old Testament, there are many accounts of warfare between Israel and Gentile nations. Pagan countries battled against Israel simply because of its covenant with God. In the book of Joshua, the first commandment God gave to the new leader of the Israelites was to possess the land of Canaan and drive out the pagan nations. Such warfare was an ongoing reality in those days. Yet, under the new covenant, the blood of Jesus Christ has become the eternal peace treaty between Jews and Gentiles. We not only have peace with God through Jesus Christ, so that we are no longer His enemies, but we also have peace with the Jewish people.

The Bible says that the *"middle wall of partition"* (Ephesians 2:14) that separated Jews and Gentiles has been removed. God has made the two groups one by uniting Jewish and Gentile believers in Jesus. This fact might not seem like much to you, but it is one of the most miraculous events in the history of the world. God told Abraham, *"Look now toward heaven, and tell the stars, if you be able to number them: and He said to him, So shall your seed be"* (Genesis 15:5). The Lord also promised him, *"In blessing I will bless you, and in multiplying I will multiply your seed as the stars of the heaven, and as the sand which is upon the sea shore"* (Genesis 22:17).

I believe God used these illustrations of the stars and the sand because He was revealing a spiritual mystery. It would have sufficed to have used sand as a comparison because grains of sand are impossible to number. Can you imagine the trillions of grains of sand that are on the earth's seashores? The sand or dirt represents the natural man, or the physical children of Israel. The stars, which are also impossible to count, represent the spiritual seed of Abraham. There are billions of stars in the solar system. Thus, these illustrations are amazing examples of God's revelation concerning His purposes! He planned to justify all nations through the Seed of Abraham.

Now to Abraham and his seed were the promises made. He said not, And to seeds, as of many; but as of one, and to your seed, which is Christ. And this I say, that the covenant, that was confirmed before of God in Christ, the law, which was four hundred and thirty years after, cannot disannul, that it should make the promise of none effect.
—Galatians 3:16–17

The Bible declares that when God referred to the *"seed,"* He was not just speaking of Abraham's physical descendants, but He was, in fact, referring to Jesus Christ. Jesus was the Seed of Abraham. God foretold that Jesus Christ, the Jewish Messiah, would be the Seed through which all nations of the earth would be justified by faith and receive eternal life.

This was the true blessing of Abraham. However, many Christians don't even pay any attention to this miraculous provision. In God's mercy, His only begotten Son became the eternal bridge that united "the sand of the sea and the stars in the heaven." The Gentiles were as far from God as the stars in the universe are from the sand on the earth—millions of miles away! But the blood of Jesus Christ has united Jew and Gentile, breaking down the wall of partition and making them into *one new man.* Hallelujah!

THE BLOOD OF JESUS CHRIST HAS BECOME THE ETERNAL PEACE TREATY BETWEEN JEWS AND GENTILES.

A NEW SPIRITUAL ENTITY

Thus, through Christ, God has literally created a new spiritual entity called the One New Man. Jew and Gentile have come together as a new creation. This is a vital aspect of our new nature! It is a combination of the spiritual DNA of Jewish and non-Jewish believers in Jesus Christ. The Bible declares that Jesus *"abolished in His flesh the enmity"* (Ephesians 2:15). What does Paul mean by *"enmity"*? He is referring to the spiritual hostility that Gentiles had toward God and His people.

Do you remember the curse that God placed on Eve after she and Adam disobeyed God? Genesis 3:15 says, *"And I will put enmity between you and the woman, and between your seed and her seed; it shall bruise your head, and you shall bruise his heel."* Those who are outside of God's covenant are the seed of the wicked one. There is an inherent enmity between the children of God and the children of the wicked one. We *"were by nature the children of wrath"* (Ephesians 2:3). This means that we were prone to reject God and violate His ordinances. The Bible says that God's ordinances were *"against us"* (Colossians 2:14) because they were contrary to our sinful nature. Actually, the law was against both Jews and Gentiles. It was against the Israelites because they could not keep the law due to their sinful nature. And it was against the Gentiles because they rejected the law due to their sinful nature.

Again, there was only one solution to this spiritual crisis—the blood of Jesus! Jesus's blood abolished the ordinances that were against us and created One New Man from two different peoples. This does not mean that Jewish people have to reject their heritage to become Christians. Neither does it mean that Gentiles must become Jews in order to be saved. It means that, from a spiritual perspective, the two are one. God no longer identifies us as separate.

There is neither Jew nor Greek, there is neither bond nor free, there is neither male nor female: for you are all one in Christ Jesus. And if you be Christ's, then are you Abraham's seed, and heirs according to the promise.   —Galatians 3:28–29

We are one in Christ! Ontologically speaking, there is no longer Jew and Gentile but a totally different entity. As one body of believers, we have all become the seed of Abraham and heirs to the promise. What is the promise? That all nations of the earth will be blessed by God.

When Jews and Gentiles come together as one in Christ, there are spiritual blessings. For years, the church has neglected this aspect of the new covenant. We are missing out on the greatest revelation from God to His people since the world began. When we apply this revelation of our new nature, it will unlock more spiritual, physical, emotional, and financial blessings than the world has ever seen.

The Bible tells us, *"The glory of this latter house shall be greater than of the former"* (Haggai 2:9). The glory of God is contained in the One New Man. It is His desire to fill the earth with His glory, but this process must begin with the church recognizing and walking in its true spiritual identity. When we do this, both Jews and Gentiles will experience healings and miracles. The blind will see. The lame will walk! As never before, the sick and oppressed will be set free by God's supernatural power. I am so excited that I want to shout! As you read this chapter, you are being healed in your body and in your mind by God's power. It is time for the church of the Lord Jesus Christ to wake up from its spiritual slumber and take its rightful place in the kingdom! God has already given us this position, but now it is time for us to walk in it.

FITLY FRAMED TOGETHER

In Ephesians 2:20–21, we read:

And are built upon the foundation of the apostles and prophets, Jesus Christ Himself being the chief corner stone; in whom all the building fitly framed together grows to a holy temple in the Lord: in whom you also are built together for a habitation of God through the Spirit.

This passage is remarkable! God says that we are built upon the foundation of the apostles and prophets. What is the significance of this statement? In the Old Testament, the house of the Lord was built upon physical foundations, but God says that He has built a spiritual house (which does not negate the physical temple), the foundations of which are apostolic and prophetic revelation. The Greek word translated "*foundation*" is *themelios*, which, in a metaphorical sense, means "the foundations, beginnings, first principles" of "an institution or a system of truth."

WILL YOU WAKE UP AND TAKE YOUR RIGHTFUL PLACE IN THE KINGDOM OF GOD, WALKING IN YOUR TRUE SPIRITUAL IDENTITY?

Thus, this *"habitation of God"* will be built on the foundation, or principles, of truth that God has established through His apostles and prophets. Jesus Christ Himself is the Chief Cornerstone. That makes His apostles and prophets the pillars. As we previously discussed, some Christians argue that the apostolic ministry has ended, but there is no biblical precedent for this claim. I believe this passage is primarily referring to the early apostles, through whom we have received the final revelation of the Scriptures. However, it also includes those apostles and prophets whom God has raised up throughout history and will raise up in these last days.

The apostolic and prophetic revelation of the One New Man is the foundation upon which the church must be established. The early church understood this revelation, and it served as an impetus for winning souls, leading to supernatural church growth. When the church in our generation embraces this truth, or first principle, we will see the same results—and even greater results than were seen in the first-century church. God is raising up apostles who will once more set forth this biblical pattern, as well as prophets who will bring this revelation to the body of Christ. Once this takes place, the people of God will be *"fitly framed together."*

The expression *"fitly framed together"* comes from the Greek word *synarmologeo*, which is a combination of three root words. The first is *sun*, which means "with," whose word origin denotes "union." The second word is *harmos*, which means "a joining" or "a joint." The third word is *lego*, which means "to say" or "to speak." The revelation behind this truth is tremendous! Once we, as believers, come to a place in which we are united as one, thinking the same things and speaking the same things, we will be joined closely together and ultimately grow into a holy temple.

In Ephesians 2:2, the Greek word for *"grows"* is *auxano*, which simply means "to increase" or "to become greater." When Jewish and Gentile believers catch this revelation, there will be exponential supernatural growth, resulting in the church becoming this holy temple that God's Spirit will inhabit. If we want to see global awakening and revival come to the church, we must be fitly joined together. We have to allow God to make us One New Man—not only ontologically, but also in our thinking, speaking, and acting. God wants to build us up!

[Jesus] *says to them, But whom say you that I am? And Simon Peter answered and said, You are the Christ, the Son of the living God. And Jesus answered and said to him, Blessed are you, Simon Barjona: for flesh and blood has not revealed it to you, but My Father which is in heaven. And I say also to you, That you are Peter, and upon this rock I will build My church; and the gates of hell shall not prevail against it. And I will give to you the keys of the kingdom of heaven: and whatsoever you shall bind on earth shall be bound in heaven: and whatsoever you shall loose on earth shall be loosed in heaven.*

—Matthew 16:15–19

Jesus said that Peter had received a revelation directly from God and that this revelation would be the *"rock"* upon which He would build His church. What was the revelation? That Jesus was *"the Christ, the Son of the Living God"*! When the complete church—both Jews and Gentiles—comes to a place where we accept the fact that Jesus is the blessing of Abraham, and that it is through His blood that the One New Man has been created, we will receive supernatural keys of authority. The gates of hell will not prevail against us! This key, or revelation, of the union of Jews and Gentiles in Christ will allow the church to take dominion on earth. When we pray, the heavens will open! When we bind the enemy, he will be bound! This is the power of a united church. This is the power of the One New Man!

> **WHEN WE ACCEPT THE FACT THAT JESUS IS THE BLESSING OF ABRAHAM, AND THAT IT IS THROUGH HIS BLOOD THAT THE ONE NEW MAN HAS BEEN CREATED, WE WILL RECEIVE SUPERNATURAL KEYS OF AUTHORITY ON EARTH.**

VICTORY PRAYER

Heavenly Father, thank You for the revelation of the One New Man! Thank You for creating a new spiritual entity by the miraculous union of Jewish and Gentile believers in Christ. May we all be "fitly framed together." As Your church applies this great revelation, may spiritual, physical, emotional, and financial blessings be unlocked for thousands of people. Let all nations of the world be blessed in Christ!

Thank You for bringing me, as one who was "far off," into Your covenant. Jesus, You are my Source of tranquility, security, safety, prosperity, and freedom from turmoil. I am are stabilized, empowered, secured, and blessed because of You. In Jesus's name, amen!

UNLOCKING THE CODE OF THE SUPERNATURAL INSIGHTS

1. What has the blood of Jesus Christ given Gentiles access to?

2. What does it mean that the *"middle wall of partition"* (Ephesians 2:14) that separated Jews and Gentiles has been removed?

3. When we apply the revelation of the One New Man, what will unlock for us?

4. How can we receive supernatural keys of authority?

17

COMPLETE IN HIM

"And you are complete in Him,
which is the head of all principality and power."
—Colossians 2:10

God is heavily concerned about the church. He paid a tremendous price to redeem His people, and, like any good businessman, He wants a return on His investment. Years ago, I began to understand and appreciate God's kingdom economy. To be healthy, vibrant, and successful, an economic system must utilize all its assets efficiently. A good market economy needs land, labor, and capital, all working in concert. In economic terms, land is defined as natural resources. Labor is defined as the workforce that exchanges its energy and time for economic gain. Capital is the equipment that is used to manufacture goods and services.

Thus, a market economy is based on competent entrepreneurs who organize the factors of production proficiently in order to gain a profit and enable the economy to grow. In God's kingdom economy, the factors of production are controlled by the King Himself. God the Father is the Master Economist, and God the Son—as the entrepreneur and King over all—has organized a perfect economy.

JESUS IS HEAD OVER ALL

The Bible says, *"For in Him* [Christ] *dwells all the fullness of the Godhead bodily"* (Colossians 2:9). After all that Jesus endured and accomplished in His life, death, resurrection, and ascension, God gave Him the highest name of authority in the universe. (See Philippians 2:6–11.) As a matter of fact, the Bible says that Jesus is *"the head of all principality and power"* (Colossians 2:10). The Greek word for *"principality"* is *arche*, among whose meanings are "principality," "rule," and "magistracy." The Greek word for *"power"* is *exousia*, which, as we noted earlier, means "authority." When these two words are used together, they imply a kingdom or government. Jesus is Head over any and all governments in the universe. He has been given sovereignty and rulership over every kingdom. This is why the Bible refers to Jesus as King of Kings and Lord of Lords. (See 1 Timothy 6:15; Revelation 17:14; 19:6.)

This is the Jesus whom we love and serve! And the Bible says that we are *"complete in Him"* (Colossians 2:10). In the original Greek, the word *"complete"* is *pleroo*, which can mean "to make full, to fill up, i.e., to fill to the full," "to cause to abound, to furnish or supply liberally," "to render full, i.e., to complete," and "to fill to the top: so that nothing shall be wanting to full measure, fill to the brim." We are members of God's kingdom economy, and God (Father, Son, and Holy Spirit) is at work within us to produce what He desires. We can work exactly the way He wants us to in Christ! Our land can be green and flourishing. We can be abundantly supplied.

How is this possible? Simple! Jesus is our Head! Many of us have never lived under a monarchy, so we don't understand the true significance of a kingdom. In a kingdom, a king is responsible for every citizen in the domain. Again, Jesus Christ is the King of God's economy, and, under His headship, rulership, and authority, we are complete.

AN "INCOMPLETE GOSPEL"

Unfortunately, many people in the body of Christ have been presented with an "incomplete gospel." As we have previously discussed, instead of being told how complete we are through the blood of Jesus Christ, we are frequently told how incomplete we are. Often, the Christian leaders and other believers who present this message have good intentions. They want people to understand their need for Christ. However, they fail to move on to the fact of our newness and sufficiency in Christ. Many pastors do not believe that they are complete in Christ, so they are not in a position to tell others about spiritual completeness.

On the other hand, sometimes leaders tell Christians that they are incomplete because they want to fuel their own "religious system." If people are made to feel insignificant and broken, they will remain dependent on a system that uses them to oil the "church machine." What do I mean by these statements? Some leaders constantly keep people in a rat race by telling them that God is *about* to bless them, that God is *about* to heal them, that God is *going to* forgive them, rather than empowering them by telling them what the Bible says: they are complete in Jesus! There is nothing lacking in Him. God has already blessed, healed, forgiven, and prospered us in Christ.

You may have been told, as I was, that you need to get the sin out of your life before God can use you. You may have been told that once you go through a series of steps, you will qualify for God's love. These ideas are simply not scriptural! Beloved, you are complete in Christ! The moment you believe this truth, you will be catapulted into victory, power, and dominion.

People often ask me, "Why doesn't the American church walk in the same dimension of the miraculous that you see in other countries?" I tell them that the difference is one of belief versus unbelief. The American church has been sold the lie that we can afford not to believe what the Scriptures say—or, at least, that we don't have to *totally* depend on God's Word—because we have so many resources available to us to meet our needs. The American church also promotes convenience rather than encouraging us to work out our salvation. As a result, many Christians are "conveniently" bound, addicted, perverted, and disobedient to God. Then, they make statements like, "I am going through a process right now!" The truth is, we either believe the Word of God or we don't. We need to be reminded of what the Scriptures say and then believe and act on what God is telling us.

Additionally, much of the Western church has not been preaching the kingdom of God. We have preached positive messages and pseudo-psychology, but we have not really exposed people to the living Christ. When I was a young pastor, I became very frustrated by the lack of change in the lives of members of my congregation. I began to earnestly seek the face of God about this matter. As I was praying, the Holy Spirit said to me, "Move out of the way!" I said, "What?" He repeated, "Move out of the way!" When I asked God for clarity, He revealed to me that I was the problem. As a leader, I was so preoccupied with giving sermons, organizing church structure, and trying to change individuals' behavior that I was inhibiting people from experiencing the fullness of Jesus Christ.

WHAT ROLE DO YOU PLAY IN GOD'S ECONOMY?

Jesus said, *"And I, if I be lifted up from the earth, will draw all men to Me"* (John 12:32). Church leaders need to move out of the way and let Jesus shine. Nothing can take the place of a supernatural encounter with Jesus Christ. He is the key to worldwide revival. Once we realize who Jesus is and understand that we are complete in Him, we will be activated to go and take dominion on earth for God's kingdom. Oh, beloved, it is time for the church to end our identity crisis! It is time for us to recognize, and be confident in, who we are! This can only happen when we put Jesus back into our preaching and teaching.

Jesus must be the Source of all our power. This is what the term *"head"* implies in Colossians 2:10. The word is translated from the Greek word *kephale*, which denotes, in a metaphorical sense, "anything supreme, chief, prominent." In a literal sense, it signifies the physical head, which houses the brain. Without the head, the body cannot function; in the same manner, without Christ, we cannot access the power we need to be victorious. Christ is not *a means* to power. He *is* the power.

> ONCE WE REALIZE WHO JESUS IS AND UNDERSTAND THAT WE ARE COMPLETE IN HIM, WE WILL BE ACTIVATED TO GO AND TAKE DOMINION ON EARTH FOR GOD'S KINGDOM.

MORE THAN CONQUERORS

Nay, in all these things we are more than conquerors through Him that loved us.
—Romans 8:37

Can I tell you a secret? Are you ready for this? You are more than a conqueror! Don't you just love how specific the Bible is? It does not say that we are "conquerors." Of course, that would be great in itself, but it is not what the verse states. The Scriptures actually say that we

are "*more than* conquerors." What does it mean to be more than a conqueror? The phrase *"more than conquerors"* comes from the Greek word
hypernikao, one of whose meanings is "to gain a surpassing victory." In
Christ, we have gained a surpassing victory! *Surpass* means "to exceed"
or "to be greater than." We have experienced a "greater-than" victory
through Jesus. This is just like fighting in a battle that we already know
we will win.

In John 14:12, Jesus said, *"Verily, verily, I say to you, he that believes on
Me, the works that I do shall he do also; and greater works than these shall he
do; because I go to My Father."* How is it possible for us to do greater works
than Jesus did? We can do them because we have the indwelling Christ
inside of us. Paul did not say that we are more than conquerors according
to our own abilities; he said that we are more than conquerors because we
are in relationship with Jesus—*"through Him that loved us."* Jesus's Spirit
and authority operate within us. Through Him, we can walk at a level of
the miraculous that exceeds that which He performed while He was on
this earth. So, when the Bible says we are more than conquerors, it is letting us know that we carry Jesus's authority. We do not operate in our own
power but in His power.

What are we more than conquerors of? Romans 8:35 tells us plainly:

*Who shall separate us from the love of Christ? shall tribulation, or
distress, or persecution, or famine, or nakedness, or peril, or sword?*

The apostle Paul is asking a rhetorical question. Tribulation, distress,
persecution, famine, nakedness, peril, and sword are *"these things"* that
Paul says we have more than conquered. These are the circumstances and
spiritual forces that seek to separate us from the love of Christ. These are
the situations of our lives that attempt to throw us into an identity crisis.
But the Bible says that, through Christ, we have a surpassing victory in all
these difficulties.

Nothing that Satan can throw at born-again believers has the power to
separate them from the love of Christ. Whatever opposition we encounter
from the devil, we face a defeated enemy! It is vital for us to understand this

truth because all real victory is born from our identity. We must realize that we are complete in Christ. He is our Source of love, power, and validation. He is the One to whom we look for strength and security, and He is the One who makes us victorious.

Do not allow the enemy to lie to you, saying that you are less than what you are. You have been given all authority in Christ. You are seated with God in heavenly places. You are not a pauper or a beggar; you are a king and a priest! (See, for example, Revelation 1:6; 5:10.) Gone are the days of being controlled by sickness. Gone are the days of being manipulated by poverty. You have the victory in Christ. You are complete in Him!

In many ways, the "church engine" that I spoke of earlier has done damage to our collective identity as the church. Some leaders are afraid that if they cultivate an atmosphere of empowerment, people will no longer need them, and they will ultimately leave their churches. The truth is, the more people are empowered through the Word of God, the more they want to engage and serve in the life of the church. And, the more people understand their identity, the more they are able to live in a way that pleases God. Furthermore, the goal of the local church is not to fill its seats but to equip its saints. When believers are equipped to walk in the supernatural, our cities, states, and nations will be permanently transformed.

We have inherited our victorious nature from our heavenly Father, through our Elder Brother, Jesus Christ. Always remember that you are complete in Christ. You are more than a conqueror through Him who loves you!

WHEN BELIEVERS ARE EQUIPPED TO WALK IN THE SUPERNATURAL, OUR CITIES, STATES, AND NATIONS WILL BE PERMANENTLY TRANSFORMED.

VICTORY PRAYER

Father, I praise and honor You because I am complete in Your Son
Jesus Christ. Through Jesus, there is nothing missing and nothing
broken in my life. I am whole. I acknowledge Jesus as the Head over
every principality and power, and over every name that is named.
In Christ, I have been given the legal right to exercise dominion
and authority in both the spiritual realm and the earthly realm.
The devil is afraid of me because of who I am in You. Demons flee
when I use the name of Jesus. I am so grateful that I am more than
a conqueror through Christ Jesus who loves me. In Jesus's name,
amen!

UNLOCKING THE CODE OF THE SUPERNATURAL INSIGHTS

1. List some meanings of *pleroo*, the Greek word translated *"complete"*
    in Colossians 2:10.

2. What are some characteristics and results of the "incomplete
    gospel"?

3. What does it mean to be "more than a conqueror"?

4. On what basis can we do greater works than Jesus did during His earthly ministry?

18

ALL THINGS NEW

"If any man be in Christ, he is a new creature ["creation," NKJV]:
old things are passed away; behold, all things are become new."
—2 Corinthians 5:17

Throughout this book, we have examined the mystery of our born-again nature. Ultimately, that mystery comes down to the word *new*. We are new creations! God has given us a brand-new life in Christ. I mentioned earlier that the Greek word translated *"new"* in 2 Corinthians 5:17 is *kainos*, which means, in regard to form, something that is "recently made, fresh... unused"; and in terms of substance, "of a new kind."

Sometimes we feel uncomfortable thinking about ourselves as new creations because we are so accustomed to identifying with the old nature. Because the old is familiar to us, we are fearful and uneasy about change. You might be amazed to discover how such fear has negatively affected your faith. Perhaps you have already made that discovery as you have been reading this book. We tend to be afraid of what we do not understand.

As I have expressed, many of the past struggles in my life occurred because I was unaware of my new identity in Christ—or because, in my uncertainty, I refused to accept my new life even after I came to understand it better. But once I embraced my newness in Christ, I accessed God's supernatural power in remarkable ways that are still unfolding today. That is why I am passionate about the message of this book. I want everyone to find and apply the keys to unlocking the power of the supernatural in their lives. If only the church would really take hold of this gospel message in all its fullness!

"GOOD ANGEL" VERSUS "BAD ANGEL"?

When I was growing up, I frequently watched cartoons. In a number of these cartoons, a character would be contemplating making a bad decision when, suddenly, two miniature figures—a "good angel" and a "bad angel"—would appear and stand on his shoulders, one on the right, and the other on the left. The good angel would to try to persuade the character not to act on this bad decision, and the bad angel would try to convince him to go ahead with it. Ultimately, the angel that the character began to yield to (usually the evil angel) would gain the upper hand, and the other angel would disappear.

These cartoons were trying to illustrate the idea that mankind has a good nature and a bad nature, and our choices are determined by one or the other. In their minds and emotions, many believers accept the idea that such a dichotomy exists within them. I call it "the-devil-made-me-do-it syndrome." Yet, is this the way it really is? As I stated previously, the truth is that a born-again believer no longer possesses a sinful nature. There are no "good and bad angels" controlling our decisions. There is only the living Christ, who dwells in our innermost being. This is what the Bible means by the phrase *"all things are become new."*

God is not telling us to engage in an internal tug-of-war with two opposing entities of good and evil. Our old sinful nature has truly been abolished in Christ. Although our body and our flesh have remained the same, our spirit-man has become new and always desires to please God. This is one of the most misunderstood theological truths in all of Christianity. Satan knows that once the church catches on to this revelation, his kingdom will experience a great reckoning. The enemy wants us to remain ignorant of who we really are. We need to fully recognize that we have received a divine nature that gives us access to God's unlimited victory and power in our lives.

GOD'S GREAT AND PRECIOUS PROMISES

According as His divine power has given to us all things that pertain to life and godliness, through the knowledge of Him that has called us to glory and virtue: whereby are given to us exceeding great and precious promises: that by these you might be partakers of the divine nature, having escaped the corruption that is in the world through lust.

—2 Peter 1:3–4

Second Corinthians 5:17 tells us that *"all things are become new."* In his second epistle, Peter expounds on this truth by letting us know that, through the promises of God's Word, we are *"partakers of the divine nature."* The Greek word for *"divine"* is *theios*, whose root, *theos*, is the term from which we derive the word *theology*. The Greek word for *"nature"* is *physis*, which refers to "the sum of innate properties and powers by which one person differs from others." God shares His own nature—His "innate properties and powers"—with us!

As I have emphasized in this book, having God's nature is an onto-logical reality for us, but we must place a claim on this reality for it to manifest in our lives. That is why 2 Peter 1:4 tells us, *"Whereby are given to us exceeding great and precious promises: that **by these** you might be partakers of the divine nature."* Partaking of God's nature is contingent upon recognizing and applying His promises. We have to understand what God says about us in His Word and exercise our faith in relation to it. Remember that God's Word is our access code to the supernatural. It is through His Word, and the Spirit's illumination of that Word to us, that we enter all the benefits and features of our new life. Too many believers have been ignorant of God's will concerning them. We have to know who we are in Christ, and the only way to know this is to study and meditate on the Scriptures.

PARTAKERS OF THE DIVINE NATURE

What does it actually signify to be a "partaker" of the divine nature? In 2 Peter 1:4, the Greek word translated *"partakers," koinonos,* is a very interesting term that has great significance for us. Among its meanings are "partner," "associate," "companion," and "sharer." We have been given a divine nature in Christ, but in order to release that nature within us, we must partner with God. Every partnership requires agreement, but many people are not living in agreement with God concerning who He is and who they are in Him. Again, their minds need to be transformed by His Word because it is the Word that will empower this partnership. God's exceedingly great and precious promises give us insight and access to His nature within us. This is an awesome truth!

WHAT ARE SOME OF GOD'S GREAT AND PRECIOUS PROMISES THROUGH WHICH YOU CAN PARTAKE OF THE DIVINE NATURE?

A BRAND-NEW LIFE

Because God has given us a brand-new life in Him, we have reason to hope. We have reason to be joyful and excited about all that He has promised us. Have you accepted what it means that the nature of God dwells within you?

Think about God's nature for a moment. He is good, loving, omniscient, pure, holy, righteous, and all-powerful. This is the very nature we have access to. This is the very nature we have been called by God to partake of. This is the very nature that dwells in our spirit-man. Our lives are not what they once were. We are no longer the same. We are unequivocally brand-new. We are fresh from the heavenly assembly line!

Remember what Paul writes in Galatians 2:19–20:

For I through the law am dead to the law, that I might live to God. I am crucified with Christ: nevertheless I live; yet not I, but Christ lives in me: and the life which I now live in the flesh I live by the faith of the Son of God, who loved me, and gave Himself for me.

Paul plainly tells us that he was crucified with Christ. From an ontological or spiritual standpoint, he was nailed to the cross with Jesus, so that his old self (by which he once defined himself) is dead. Paul then says, *"Nevertheless I live."* Because he has been raised with Christ, it is not the old Paul who is now living, but Christ who is living in him. Most people struggle with this concept because religion has taught us to try to fight the evil inside us. We have been taught to say things like, "My flesh rose up, and I sinned" or "I lost my religion and did something I shouldn't have." Such expressions exalt the old nature to a position of prominence and influence in our lives. We must continually keep in mind that the old man has been put to death by the power of the Holy Spirit.

If you need additional proof of this fact, consider Colossians 3:3: *"For you are dead, and your life is hidden with Christ in God."* Our old man has been put to death, and we are a new creation. There is no "good angel" and "bad angel" inside of us—there is just Jesus. Of course, I am not suggesting that we don't have to contend with our unregenerate flesh. Paul deals with this topic in great detail in Romans 7. But he attributes the evil that arises in his life to sin that dwells inside his flesh: *"Now if I do that I would not, it is no more I that do it, but sin that dwells in me"* (Romans 7:20).

The more we yield to the life of God within us, the more we can take dominion over the power of our sinful flesh. This is what it means to have a new life. We now live from a position of power, not from a position of weakness. Before we were born again, we obeyed the dictates of our sinful nature. Now that we are in Christ, we yield to the life of His Spirit. We live through His power, and the flesh is merely a roadblock to our righteousness. I thank God that the Holy Spirit is a spiritual bulldozer with the power to demolish sin in our lives!

 THE HOLY SPIRIT IS A SPIRITUAL BULLDOZER WITH THE POWER TO DEMOLISH SIN IN OUR LIVES!

A BRAND NEW DAY

As we close this book, I want to encourage you that today is a brand-new day for you! If Jesus Christ is the Lord of your life, God has made you a new person. (If you have not yet made this commitment, you will have another opportunity to accept Christ into your life at the end of this chapter.) It doesn't matter what the enemy has tried to tell you—today is the day that the Lord has made, and you can rejoice and be glad in it! The power of Jesus Christ resonates in your spirit. The same Spirit who raised Jesus from the dead lives in you, and He will give life to your mortal body.

This is the mystery! This is the code of the supernatural that we have been unlocking throughout these chapters. We have an eternal God who loves us and sent His Son to die for us. The moment we were born again, our lives took on brand-new meaning. We are now God's sons and daughters. He desires to display His grace, mercy, love, and supernatural power through us. We are no longer victims, no longer defeated, no longer broken. We have been restored to life, and God wants to use us for His glory. Today is our day!

You may say, "Pastor Kynan, you don't know what I've been through!" I say to you, "You don't know what *He's* been through!" Jesus came to earth from eternity, clothed Himself in humanity, suffered on a cross, died, descended into hell, defeated Satan, was raised triumphantly from the dead, and ascended to heaven again so that you could have eternal life. He went through great lengths because of His love for you. You owe Him a debt of gratitude that you could never repay. All you can do is partake of what He has made available to you. All you can do is allow Him to live in and through you. This is your portion. This is your inheritance.

You are not incomplete but complete. You are not unrighteous but righteous. You are not old but new. You are born again from an incorruptible seed. You have divine life at work within you. Do you understand what all this means? Sin can no longer reign in your life. You are holy, righteous, redeemed, saved, sanctified, empowered, faithful, and blessed, all because of the One who dwells inside you.

Get up! Start walking like the new person that God's Word says you are. God has given you authority over the enemy, and He has given you the power to exercise that authority, which is inherent in your new nature. No more excuses; no more fear! Now is the time for the children of God to be made manifest.

This is a new day in the history of the church. We are at the beginning of a supernatural revolution. This revolution begins with you. It starts the moment you reject the lies of the enemy and exchange them for God's unchanging truth.

To whom God would make known what is the riches of the glory of this mystery among the Gentiles; which is Christ in you, the hope of glory. —Colossians 1:27

"Christ in you" is the supernatural mystery that was hidden for ages— and is still being buried in the caverns of religion and tradition in our

modern age. "Christ in us" is what the church needs in order to overcome sin, sickness, poverty, and defeatism. We must become conscious of, and intimate with, the indwelling Christ. Once we do, we will continuously walk in the supernatural.

In fact, "a new day" is really an understatement in terms of what you will experience when you assimilate these truths into your heart and mind. Never again will you be manipulated by fear. Never again will you be bound by the law or caught in the vicious cycle of striving for God's acceptance. You will no longer question whether God loves you. You will be secure in your new identity in Christ, and this identity will empower you to live the life God originally intended for you. Just like Adam and Eve before the fall, you will walk in intimate fellowship with the Lord. You will operate in revelation knowledge, wisdom, and spiritual understanding. The power of the Holy Spirit will release you from the bondage of sin, shame, and condemnation. Demons will no longer be able to attach themselves to you or oppress you because you will have an overwhelming consciousness of God's love and delivering presence. Rise, take up your bed, and walk! From this day forward, there are no more limitations. Unlock the code of the supernatural in your life because today is a brand-new day!

GET UP! START WALKING LIKE THE NEW PERSON
THE WORD OF GOD SAYS YOU ARE.
NOW IS THE TIME FOR THE CHILDREN OF
GOD TO BE MADE MANIFEST.

PRAYER OF SALVATION

Heavenly Father, I recognize that I am a sinner in desperate need of a Savior. I believe that Jesus Christ is Your Son. I believe that He suffered on the cross and died for me, descended into hell and defeated Satan, and now sits at Your right hand praying for me so that I may have abundant life. I am sorry for my sins; I repent of them and renounce them. Through the blood of Christ, I ask You to forgive me of all of my sins—those that are known to me and those that are unknown to me.

I receive Jesus as my Lord and Savior, and I give Him complete control over my life. I want to live for You from my innermost being and in every area of my life. I renounce Satan and all of his wicked works. I divorce myself from his evil influence. Lord, I recognize that I cannot live for You in my own strength. I ask You to fill me with Your precious Holy Spirit and give me the gift of speaking in other tongues, as the Spirit gives utterance, as the initial evidence of a transformed life. I ask this in the name of Your Son, Jesus Christ, amen!

UNLOCKING THE CODE OF THE SUPERNATURAL INSIGHTS

1. What is "the-devil-made-me-do-it syndrome"? What is the truth regarding this mindset?

2. What are some meanings of the Greek word *koinonos*, which is translated as *"partakers"* in 2 Peter 1:4? Why is this word so significant for us?

3. List some of the attributes of God's nature that we have access to because His nature dwells within our spirit-man.

4. What is the supernatural mystery that was hidden for ages and is still being buried in the caverns of religion and tradition in our modern age?

ABOUT THE AUTHOR

Dr. Kynan T. Bridges is the senior pastor of Grace & Peace Global Fellowship in Tampa, Florida. With a profound revelation of the Word of God and a dynamic teaching ministry, Dr. Bridges has revolutionized the lives of many in the body of Christ. Through his practical approach to applying the deep truths of the Word of God, he reveals the authority and identity of the new covenant believer.

God has placed on Dr. Bridges a particular anointing for understanding and teaching the Scriptures, along with the gifts of prophecy and healing. Dr. Bridges and his wife, Gloria, through an apostolic anointing, are committed to equipping the body of Christ to live in the supernatural every day and to fulfill the Great Commission. It is the desire of Dr. Bridges to see the nations transformed by the unconditional love of God.

A highly sought speaker and published author of a number of books, his previous books with Whitaker House include *School of the Miraculous*, *Invading the Heavens*, *Unmasking the Accuser*, *The Power of Prophetic Prayer*, and *Kingdom Authority*. Dr. Bridges is a committed husband, a mentor, and a father of five beautiful children: Ella, Naomi, Isaac, Israel, and Anna.

Welcome to Our House!

We Have a Special Gift for You

It is our privilege and pleasure to share in your love of Christian books. We are committed to bringing you authors and books that feed, challenge, and enrich your faith.

To show our appreciation, we invite you to sign up to receive a specially selected **Reader Appreciation Gift**, with our compliments. Just go to the Web address at the bottom of this page.

God bless you as you seek a deeper walk with Him!

WE HAVE A GIFT FOR YOU. VISIT:

whpub.me/nonfictionthx

WHITAKER
HOUSE